STUFF EVERY CHEESE LOVER SHOULD KNOW

Alexandra Jones

QUIRK BOOKS

PHILADELPHIA

Library of Congress Cataloging in Publication Number: 2020904606

ISBN: 978-1-68369-238-6

Printed in China

Typeset in Laca, Brandon Grotesque, Adobe Garamond, and Akzidenz-Grotesk

Cover designed by Elissa Flanigan
Interior designed by Molly Rose Murphy
Illustrations by Lucy Engelman
Production management by John J. McGurk

Quirk Books
215 Church Street
Philadelphia, PA 19106
quirkbooks.com

10 9 8 7 6 5 4 3 2 1

For Stef and Sue

EATING CHEESE

COOKING WITH CHEESE

NEXT-LEVEL CHEESE LOVER STUFF

INTRODUCTION

If you've ever dug into a ripe oozy wheel of Camembert, been tantalized by the pungent aroma of a whiffy washed-rind cheese, or crunched down on the tyrosine crystals in a savory toffee-like wedge of long-aged Gouda, you know that cheese holds a power over humans unlike any other food. It is sustenance, yes, but it's so much more: an artistic statement from the maker, an expression of a specific place, a living thing that changes over time. Cheese contains multitudes.

As the twentieth-century author and intellectual Clifton Fadiman famously quipped:

> *"A cheese may disappoint. It may be dull, it may be naive, it may be over-sophisticated. Yet it remains cheese, milk's leap toward immortality."*

Although we usually only hear the last few words of this quote, I appreciate the entire thought, which allows us to consider not only centuries-old icons like Parmigiano-Reggiano and Brie de Meaux but also the everyday blocks that are many people's first, only, or most beloved experiences of cheese.

Your formative fromage may have been satiny Velveeta enveloping macaroni, umami-packed Cheeto powder licked from your thumb and forefinger, or an American cheese single melted between two slices of bread or over a steaming bowl of Shin Ramyun. My love of cheese began when I was a kid, eating bright-orange bricks of extra-sharp cheddar from the grocery store. Cut into squares and stacked with slices of garlicky dill pickles atop Triscuits, it was the centerpiece of my favorite after-school snack.

But if your knowledge of cheese begins with Babybel and ends with mozzarella sticks, you're seriously missing out. Getting a cheese education after a lifetime of the supermarket stuff is like when *The Wizard of Oz* goes from black and white to color. It's the first sip of a heady IPA after only drinking Coors Light. It's that moment you tasted a *real* tomato, the sweet-savory juices dripping down your chin, warm from the August heat. It's a whole world of tantalizing flavors, compelling textures, passionate personalities, dynamic cultures, deep histories, singular places, and fascinating stories. And it tastes so, so good.

This book is for anyone who wants to take the first step from casual cheese eater to budding connoisseur and beyond. Everyone's love of cheese has to start somewhere. Now, let's take it to new heights.

CHEESE
BASICS

WHAT IS CHEESE?

No matter where they're from, nearly all cheeses are made with the same four basic ingredients:

MILK	RENNET
CULTURES	SALT

Humans began raising animals—first goats and sheep, and then cattle—for meat and fiber around ten thousand years ago. Shortly thereafter, they figured out how to milk those animals.

Initially, fluid milk was used to feed children only, because they possessed the ability to digest lactose, a sugar in milk that adults could not process. (Over millennia, genetic mutations in certain populations with a history of dairying in northern Europe, regions of East and West Africa, Central Asia, and parts of South Asia have allowed adults to retain this ability.)

But over time, humans learned how to make milk into a safe, storable, portable, and delicious food source. The cheesemaking process removes much if not all of the lactose, making fermented dairy products foundational foods in many parts of the world. In the pages that follow, we'll learn more about the process that turns these four ingredients into cheese.

TERMS EVERY CHEESE LOVER SHOULD KNOW

Affinage: In cheesemaking, this French word, meaning "refinement," refers to the process of aging cheese to its ideal ripeness.

Artisan: Describes cheeses produced using traditional methods, typically on a small scale, by a skilled cheesemaker.

Bloomy rind: A category of cheese named for the way *Penicillium candidum* mold "blooms" in snowy white tufts on the wheel's surface. Examples include Camembert and Brie.

Casein: The primary milk protein that is manipulated in cheesemaking.

Cheese cave: A cool, high-humidity aging space for cheese.

Coagulation: The process of changing milk from liquid to solid.

Commodity cheeses: Generic cheeses produced on an industrial scale, typically for long-term storage or processing.

Cream line: A soft, liquid-like layer that forms between the rind and the paste of bloomy-rind cheeses as the cheese ripens and proteins break down during aging.

Cultures: Microbes that lower pH and develop flavors and textures in a cheese by converting lactose to lactic acid and breaking down proteins. Today, cheesemakers almost always purchase freeze-dried powdered cultures from big biotech companies, but for much of human history, these cultures occurred naturally in the milk and in the air and soil on the farm.

Curd: Coagulated milk.

Double/triple crème: Cheeses in which additional cream is added to the milk before coagulation begins.

Eyes: Tiny air holes in the paste (such as in Swiss cheese). A cheese without eyes is called a *blind cheese*.

Farmstead: Describes cheese made on the same farm where the milk was produced.

Geotrichum: A yeast responsible for the wrinkly, brainlike rinds on certain bloomy cheeses, such as Selles-sur-Cher, Valençay, and Bonne Bouche.

Hooping: The process of draining whey from the curds and forming them into wheels, which gives cheeses their shape.

Lactic: Term used to describe milk-like flavors in a cheese. It's also used to describe soft-ripened or bloomy-rind cheeses that are coagulated primarily with lactic acid produced by starter cultures and just a little rennet, such as Crottin de Chavignol and Sainte-Maure.

Lactic acid: A by-product of starter cultures consuming lactose. Lactic acid is what gives fresh cheeses and yogurts their tangy flavor.

Lactose: A sugar in milk that is converted into lactic acid during cheesemaking. Individuals who are lactose intolerant are unable to fully digest this sugar.

Molds: Microscopic fungi that grow on the rinds and cut surfaces of cheeses.

Native cultures: Naturally occurring microbes in the air, soil, or milk that the cheesemaker has captured from their unique environment (for more, see page 38). The cheesemaker cultures samples of milk from their favorite animals. The most vigorous sample becomes the *grandmother culture*, which is used to culture each batch made that season.

Paste: The portion of the cheese inside the rind.

Pasteurization: The process of heating milk to kill potential pathogens and increase shelf life.

Raw milk: Milk that has not been pasteurized; also used to describe cheeses made with unpasteurized milk.

Rennet: Enzymes that are added to milk to help it coagulate into curd.

Rind: The outer surface that develops on a wheel of aged cheese. Some cheeses, like block cheddar and fresh cheeses such as chèvre, are rindless.

Ripe: Describes a cheese that is ready to eat.

Ruminants: Animals such as cows, goats, sheep, water buffalo, and camels with four stomachs that chew their cud, or regurgitate food for further breakdown. These animals can digest vegetation that humans can't, and the milk that many of them produce makes delicious cheese.

Surface ripened: Describes cheeses that ripen from the outside in, like bloomy- and washed-rind cheeses.

Terroir: This term, which comes from the French word meaning "earth" or "soil," refers to the unique combination of characteristics possessed by a cheese made in a specific place.

Tomme: A generic term for a type of natural rind cheese typically made in the French and Swiss Alps but used as a template for cheeses around the world with a variety of different characteristics.

Turophile (or tyrophile): From the ancient Greek *tyros*, meaning "cheese," a lover or connoisseur of cheese (synonymous with *caseophile*).

Tyrosine: An amino acid found in casein that sometimes creates crunchy crystals in long-aged cheeses such as Parmigiano-Reggiano.

Washed rind: Describes a cheese that's been bathed in a salt brine in order to cultivate desirable microbes (and keep away bad ones) on its surface. These cheeses are also referred to as *smear-ripened* cheeses.

Wheel: An uncut cheese in its original form; typically refers to round cheeses but is also used to describe cheeses that are made in other shapes.

Whey: The protein-rich liquid by-product of cheese-making, left over after the curds have been cut.

HOW CHEESE IS MADE

At its most basic, cheesemaking is the act of capturing the fats, proteins, and minerals in milk and removing the liquid to concentrate these nutrients for efficiency, portability, and storability.

The conversion of fresh milk to finished cheese can take anywhere from one day to several years. There are many variables along the way: the type of rennet and cultures used, the moisture level, and conditions in the aging environment. But the basic steps are as follows.

1. WARMING THE MILK

The number-one factor in determining the quality of a finished cheese is the quality of the milk (see page 30). Raw (aka unpasteurized) milk is piped into a cheese-making vat—basically a big stainless-steel pot with a paddle that stirs the milk. The milk may be heated to pasteurize it, or it may be warmed to prepare it for the addition of starter cultures.

2. CULTURING

The cheesemaker adds microbes known as *starter cultures* to the milk, which convert lactose into lactic acid and thus lower the pH of the milk, along with *secondary* or *adjunct cultures*, which will influence the cheese's character during the aging step.

3. COAGULATION

This is the step during which milk turns into a semi-solid known as *curd*. The cheesemaker adds rennet, an ingredient that causes coagulation. Along with the increased acidity from the starter cultures, rennet makes molecules of casein—the most important protein in cheesemaking—adhere around the fat and moisture in the milk to form curd. When the curd has the bouncy-yet-solid texture of silken tofu, sort of like a milky Jell-O, it's ready to be cut.

4. CUTTING THE CURDS

The cheesemaker uses a multibladed knife called a *curd harp* to cut the curd into little pieces. The cuts expose more of the curd's surface area and release *whey*, a liquid by-product of cheesemaking. Milk is around 87 percent water, so most of its initial weight is lost during the cheesemaking process. (If you've ever wondered why a piece of cheese is so much smaller yet more expensive than a gallon of milk, this is why.) At this point, fresh cheeses such as chèvre, *fromage blanc*, or mozzarella will be hung in cheesecloth to drain or be stretched and shaped.

5. HOOPING, DRAINING, AND CURING

To make most cheeses (except fresh varieties), the cheesemaker *hoops* the cheese, pouring the cut curds into molds known as *cheese forms*. These molds contain tiny holes that allow liquid to drain away from the curds. Once in the forms, the curds drain, either under their own weight or with the help of a press. When draining is done, the wheels are allowed to dry and cured with salt.

6. AGING

At this point, the product can technically be called cheese. But it doesn't taste like much, and its texture is rubbery and uninspiring. It's *green*—meaning young or unripened. Most cheeses are then stashed in a *cheese cave*—a cool, humid space where the cheese can mature—for anywhere from a few weeks to several years. With time, the right conditions, and regular care, the wheels will develop into unique, lively, and luscious finished cheeses.

AFFINAGE: FINISHING SCHOOL FOR CHEESE

During the aging process, cheeses get all kinds of special treatment. The care that a cheese receives after cheesemaking is complete, but before it goes home with you, is called *affinage*, which is a French word that translates to "refinement."

Factors like the size of the wheel and conditions such as humidity, temperature, and ventilation in the aging cave all play a part in how the cheese matures— and that's before any physical intervention from the cheesemaker, or *affineur*. Depending on the type of cheese, it may undergo several of these processes.

Exposure to air: First, the cheese must form a rind, the outer crust that protects the wheel's interior. For this to happen, it must be exposed to air. (The exceptions are rindless varieties such as fresh cheeses, brined cheeses, some blues, which are wrapped in foil to keep a rind from forming, and some cheddars, which age in vacuum-sealed plastic.) The rate and manner in which a cheese ages is dictated by the amount of moisture it will ultimately contain; soft, moist cheeses such as Brie ripen much more quickly than hard, dry ones, like Parmigiano-Reggiano.

Flipping or rotating: In the aging cave, cheeses must be flipped or rotated regularly to ensure that moisture is distributed evenly.

Surface treatments: The exterior of a natural-rind cheese is often brushed or scrubbed to distribute or reduce molds growing on the surface. These molds can attract cheese mites, tiny organisms that can further develop the rinds in some cheeses. Mites can damage the rind or contribute to off-aromas if left unchecked, but most cheesemakers see them as helpers in the development of a cheese's character. Other cheeses are bathed or rubbed with a salt brine, which promotes the growth of good microbes on the rind and helps keep undesirable bugs at bay.

Piercing: Blue cheeses must be pierced periodically during aging—around four dozen times per wheel from both the top and the bottom—to let in air. Without oxygen, blue mold won't grow in the interior of the cheese.

CHEESE MATH: FACTS AND FIGURES

Impress your friends and other cheese lovers at your next gathering or cheese tasting (see page 131) with these stats.

- According to *The Oxford Companion to Cheese*, it takes 10 pounds of cow's or goat's milk to make 1 pound of cheese. Because sheep's milk is higher in fat, only 5 pounds are needed to make 1 pound of cheese.

- These days, Americans prefer to eat their dairy. According to the Economic Research Service of the U.S. Department of Agriculture, although consumption of fluid milk declined 25 percent between 2000 and 2018, consumption of cheese (not including American or cottage) increased more than 33 percent during the same period. Excluding cottage cheese, Americans ate 38.15 pounds of cheese per capita in 2018.

- Nearly 1,500 varieties of cheese are produced in France, according to *The Oxford Companion to Cheese*. The nation boasts 45 protected cheese styles, more than any other country in the world. (For more about protected cheeses, see page 80.)

- Although cheesemaking culture in Japan is relatively new, the country has more than 300 small-scale cheesemakers operating there, according to the Japanese Cheese Co.

- The Wisconsin Milk Marketing Board reported that the United States topped world cheese production in 2018 with 13 billion pounds produced, of which 3.4 billion were produced in Wisconsin alone. Germany was next, with 5.4 billion pounds; France third, with 4.5 billion; Italy fourth, with 3 billion; and Russia fifth, with 2.1 billion.

- NPR reported in early 2019 that America's stash of commodity cheese in cold storage reached 1.4 billion pounds in 2018—the highest it's been in a century.

HIGHLIGHTS FROM CHEESE HISTORY

8500 BCE: Goats in the Fertile Crescent are the first livestock to be domesticated by humans early in the Neolithic Revolution. They're initially raised for meat and fiber, not milk.

7000 BCE: Cattle are first domesticated in western Anatolia (modern-day Turkey).

6500 BCE: After generations of livestock breeding and domestication—coupled with a population explosion in the Levant that depleted resources—people turn to milking sheep, cows, and goats as a food source that utilizes grazing lands not suited for crops. Around the same time, pottery-making techniques are developed, which allows humans to store milk, ferment it, and drain off whey—making cheese possible.

4500 BCE: By this time, the cheesemaking culture that originated in the Fertile Crescent has taken hold across Europe, in the Mediterranean, and through Western Asia down to India.

2500 to 1250 BCE: The Hittites in central Anatolia include a fight with cheeses—as weapons, not opponents—as part of the entertainment at one of their religious festivals.

150 BCE to 450 CE: The Romans produce the earliest recorded smoked cheese, with the best wheels found in, and named for, the Velabrum, the city's bustling food marketplace.

774 CE: Brie de Meaux, produced on farmsteads around the Abbaye du Jouare outside Paris, earns an important fan: the emperor Charlemagne, who placed regular orders for the iconic soft-ripened cheese.

1184: Gouda, a cheese that would become synonymous with the Netherlands in the seventeenth century, first enters the historical record.

Late 13th century: The earliest record of a macaroni-and-cheese-type dish appears in the anonymously authored Neapolitan cookbook *Liber de coquina*, according to the food writer and historian Clifford A. Wright. Called *de lasanis*—which sounds an awful lot like lasagna—the dish consists of boiled squares of fermented pasta dough tossed with grated cheese.

1585: Following Spanish colonization, the first cheeses are produced in Mexico, using sheep's milk.

1623: The first dairy cows arrive in what is now the United States, brought along with East Anglian colonizers to Plymouth Colony.

1854: French scientist Louis Pasteur discovers that yeasts are responsible for fermentation—and that heating products like wine, beer, and milk could halt microbial activity without damaging flavor and quality.

1919: Cabot Creamery, the farmer-owned New England dairy famed for its cheddar, is founded in Vermont.

1937: Kraft Dinner—the first boxed mac and cheese product, consisting of noodles with a package of grated cheese attached—debuts in the United States.

1964: The New York World's Fair introduces the U.S. to Swiss fondue, the tradition of enjoying crusty bread dipped in warm, luscious melted Alpine cheese.

1970s: Women like Capriole's Judy Schad, Cypress Grove's Mary Keene, Alison Hooper of Vermont Butter and Cheese, and Laura Chenel of Laura Chenel's Chèvre pioneer a new era in American cheesemaking.

2018: Archaeologists from the University of Catania and the University of Cairo identify the earliest Egyptian cheese in the tomb of a high-ranking official. It's 3,200 years old.

GOOD MILK MAKES GOOD CHEESE

Milk is the main ingredient in cheese by far—like 99.9 percent. But what makes great milk?

Milk is an emulsion of fats, proteins, and sugar suspended in water. These solids determine the quality of the milk. The sugar, lactose, is what feeds the cultures during the cheesemaking process. Fat and casein, a protein, are what cheesemakers manipulate when making cheese. As proteins are broken down by enzymes—which may be naturally occurring, added by the cheesemaker, or produced by microbes during cheesemaking—the resulting amino acids and peptides create flavors and aromas. Fat carries lots of flavor, too, in the form of lipid-soluble compounds that make cheese smell or taste a certain way. As enzymes break down the triglycerides in milk's fat, fatty acids are released, contributing to flavor, aroma, and the overall character of the cheese. Fat and protein affect texture, too: cheeses with lower fat and higher protein are typically firmer, whereas cheeses higher in fat are usually softer and melt better.

For these reasons, the milk you pour on your morning cereal and the milk that makes great cheese aren't the same. Milk for cheesemaking must be very fresh, ideally pumped into the vat straight from the storage tank after milking (even a day of refrigeration causes cold-loving microbes to grow and affect the finished cheese's flavor). It typically has more fat and protein per gallon than fluid milk, resulting in a better yield. Milk that makes the best-tasting cheese is unpasteurized, too. Pasteurization kills off beneficial microbes like lactic acid bacteria, as well as flavor compounds and enzymes naturally present in milk—which help develop deeper flavors and aromas.

Feeding cows a grass-based diet also creates tastier cheese. In a 2013 study led by the Wisconsin Department of Agriculture, researchers found that cheese and butter made from the milk of pasture-raised animals had creamier textures, more golden color, and more complex, lively flavors and aromas than products made from conventionally produced milk. Cows that eat grass are healthier and give milk richer in omega-3 fatty acids than that of animals fed corn and soybeans.

Milk characteristics vary from breed to breed. Jersey cow's milk in particular is very high in fat, which makes for rich cheese. Heritage breeds like Ayreshire, Milking Shorthorn, and Brown Swiss also make rich milk conducive to cheesemaking.

MILK TYPES

One of the most basic ways to categorize cheeses is by milk type. In the U.S., cow's milk cheeses are by far the most common. Goat's and sheep's milk cheeses are more prevalent in parts of Europe and Western Asia, and water buffalo are milked throughout Asia. These are the most common ruminants whose milk is made into cheese. (Though it's difficult—and often very expensive—to get your hands on, cheese is also made from the milk of moose, yaks, camels, and donkeys.)

Cow: Sweet, creamy, and lactic, cow's milk is versatile and abundant; modern dairy cows produce an average of 8 gallons of milk per day. This milk has fewer short-chain fatty acids than goat's milk (these account for the "goat-y" flavor of stored goat's milk and some goat cheeses that can be off-putting). When we talk about milk generally in this book, we're referring to cow's milk unless otherwise noted.

Goat: Though goats don't really chow down on tin cans like they do in cartoons, they do eat the leaves of many trees and shrubs in addition to grasses. As a result, wild herbs and plants in a region will influence the flavor of goat's milk and cheese. Goat's milk is less sweet than cow's milk and contains more short-chain fatty acids, giving it a distinct flavor that results in tangy, light fresh cheeses and earthy aged cheeses. Because goat's milk has smaller fat globules and a slightly different protein structure than cow's milk, some people may find it easier to digest.

Sheep: Sheep produce only a tenth of the milk in a year that cows do, but their rich, buttery milk is prized for cheesemaking. Because it contains twice the fat and 70 percent more protein than cow's milk, half as much sheep's milk is needed to produce the same amount of cheese. Signature sheep's milk cheeses are Roquefort, Manchego, feta, and Pecorino.

Water buffalo: Though Italy is known for its ultra-rich mozzarella di bufala, the vast majority of the world's water buffalo are raised across Asia. Their milk is made into cheese in India, China, Indonesia, and the Philippines.

GET IT TOGETHER: COAGULATION

To separate the liquid in milk from those fats and proteins, it must undergo coagulation, the process of turning liquid milk into curds.

Casein proteins are suspended in milk within structures called *micelles*, which are covered in hairlike particles that prevent them from clotting together. They're negatively charged and repel each other, similar to the effect of pointing the negative ends of two magnets together. But clotting is exactly what the cheesemaker wants, so she overcomes this with one of the following three methods.

Acid: Acid-set cheeses are some of the simplest to make; examples are soft, fresh varieties like chèvre and cottage cheese. The addition of an acidic ingredient like lemon juice or vinegar, or the production of lactic acid during fermentation, will neutralize the negative charge of the micelles and allow them to form into curds.

Acid and heat: When milk is heated, its whey proteins are denatured, which means their tightly wound structures unravel so that they can grab on to each other. When acid is introduced, these denatured proteins can also bind to casein. Cheeses made this way include ricotta, queso blanco, and paneer; they are a bit firmer in structure than acid-set cheeses.

Rennet: The enzymes in rennet, whether animal, vegetable, or microbial (see "What Is Rennet?," page 36), effectively "cut" the hairs off the casein micelles. This allows the proteins to come together and form a gel-like curd. Most aged cheeses are rennet-set.

WHAT IS RENNET?

Rennet consists of enzymes that turn milk into curds. It takes only a tiny amount of rennet to coagulate a batch of cheese. There are three main types.

Animal: The original rennet! An enzyme called *chymosin* is found in the lining of the fourth stomach, or *abomasum*, of young ruminants to help them coagulate and digest their mother's milk until they are old enough to eat grass. The enzyme is extracted and used in cheesemaking. It's theorized that the earliest dairy farmers thousands of years ago may have observed curds in the stomachs of calves, lambs, or kids, and that this led to the discovery of rennet.

Vegetable: Rennet can be derived from plants such as fig trees, stinging nettles, and members of the thistle family. These plants, along with caper leaves, mallow, and ground ivy, contain enzymes that act similarly to chymosin on casein micelles. Vegetable rennet takes longer to coagulate and produces softer, more acidic curds than animal rennet.

Microbial: These types of rennet can be produced in different ways—and which is used in a cheese whose ingredients include "microbial rennet" is often unclear.

Microbial recombinant rennet, or fermentation-produced chymosin (FPC), is produced by injecting bacteria or fungi with the genetic material (RNA) of chymosin from a calf and fermenting the bacteria. The chymosin that's created is then purified, which makes FPC technically non-GMO based on some regulatory definitions. As a coagulant, FPC works almost identically to animal rennet, is more effective than the real thing, and is much cheaper to produce. Around 80 percent of commercial cheese in the U.S. and U.K. is made with FPC.

The other type of microbial rennet is produced by growing and fermenting molds such as *Rhizomucor miehei*, which produce enzymes that can coagulate milk. This rennet is produced with no GMOs but isn't quite as good at coagulating milk as animal rennet or FPC and may contribute bitter flavors to the cheese.

An easy way to avoid GMOs in cheese is to seek products from small-scale producers using animal rennet. If you seek non-GMO, vegetarian cheeses, look for the terms "Certified Organic" or "Non-GMO Project Certified" on the label. When it comes to artisan cheeses, ask your monger—or better yet, seek out a local cheesemaker at your farmers' market and have a conversation about what they're using and why.

MICROBES 101

Microbes are the invisible heroes of the cheese world. Over millennia, cheesemakers figured out how to create conditions that would promote the growth of "good" bacteria, or the ones that impart desirable characteristics to cheese, and eliminate "bad" bacteria—pathogens that can cause illness—that may have been present in unpasteurized milk. Culturing milk, which creates an acidic environment in which bad microbes can't thrive, is the first step. Adding salt (on the exterior or mixing into the curds before hooping), reducing moisture through draining and pressing, aging, and washing rinds to keep undesirable molds from growing are other methods a cheesemaker can use.

Today, most cheesemakers purchase standardized, premade cultures to make their products: a blend of starter cultures to acidify the milk, plus secondary or adjunct cultures to create certain flavors or textures, like the bubble-forming bacteria responsible for the eyes in some Alpine cheeses or the mold that creates vibrant veins in blue cheese.

But a cheese isn't defined only by the cultures the cheesemaker adds. Microbes that affect the unique character of a cheese are naturally present at almost every step: in the soil, in raw milk, in the cheese room, and in the cave. The resulting characteristics of such environmental influences—which also include climate, terrain, and agricultural practices—are what's referred to as terroir. Unless a cheesemaker is using pasteurized milk exclusively, the process involves finding a balance between added cultures and naturally occurring microbes. This isn't a bad thing—in fact, it's what makes each cheese unique.

Native cultures can be maintained by saving part of the milk or whey from the previous day's batch of cheese and using it to culture the next day's milk. Traditional wooden implements like milk pails and bowls can be inoculated with beneficial microflora, which begin to grow when new milk is added. To create cultures from her creamery's signature microbes, a cheesemaker will hand-milk samples from the animals in her herd that give her the best, richest milk. This raw milk is put into sterile jars and allowed to *clabber*, or culture naturally—meaning the lactic acid bacteria already present in the milk and in the environment will create lactic acid and multiply, thickening the milk and giving it a yogurt-like tang. The cheesemaker will select the sample with the best flavor, then use it to inoculate pasteurized milk. This becomes the *grandmother culture* for that season's cheese, a microbial mix that's unlike any other in the world.

MOISTURE IN CHEESE

Moisture is a defining characteristic of cheese. After all, every cheese starts its life as a liquid—milk—and the cheesemaking process, at its most basic, is the process of separating out the solids (fats, proteins, minerals, and lactose). How much moisture remains in the finished product can significantly affect the taste, texture, and appearance of the cheese. Think of the difference, for example, between a tender ball of fresh mozzarella and a crumbly hunk of long-aged Parmigiano-Reggiano. Both started as milk, but the years that the latter spent aging and slowly losing moisture turned it into quite a different product.

One of the biggest factors that determines the lifespan of a cheese is how much moisture it contains. A large wheel that's had most of the moisture pressed out can age for much longer, giving it the chance to develop deeper flavors, a firm texture, and desirable traits like tyrosine crystals (see page 19). A softer, younger cheese contains more of the milk's original water content and can't be aged for nearly as long.

Too much moisture in an aged cheese can allow microbes to grow and create off-flavors in the finished product, or it may cause the cheese to ripen more quickly, which can affect its body and texture. It also takes much more milk to make the same amount by weight of a drier aged cheese than a higher-moisture one.

Moisture is also indirectly related to how much lactose remains in the finished cheese. Around 97 percent of the lactose in milk drains out in whey during the cheesemaking process, and what remains is slowly consumed by lactic acid bacteria during aging—meaning that while most aged cheeses contain near-undetectable levels of lactose, the ones with the least lactose are harder, drier varieties that have hung out in the cave for several months or more.

In addition to flavor, moisture content is an important consideration when choosing to use a given cheese in cooking. For example, you'd never grate a log of fresh chèvre or a wheel of Brie over a pizza—it just wouldn't work. Firmer cheeses may be easier to grate, but they can also be crumbly and shorter in texture than cheeses with higher moisture and fat. Although fat content also plays a big role in a cheese's texture, as a general rule, the softer a cheese is, the more moisture it contains, and the firmer it is, the drier it is.

Moisture is also a key factor that determines how well a cheese melts. Generally, a higher-moisture cheese melts better than a drier one (for more, see "Why Some Cheeses Melt Differently," page 78).

CHEESE OUTERWEAR

Some cheeses get an extra outer layer to help with rind development. This addition may protect the cheese while it ages, offer structural support, or simply add flavor and visual appeal. Some of these additions, like ash or herbs, become part of an edible rind, whereas others, like wax, bark, leaves, or cloth, must be removed before the cheese can be eaten.

ASH

Valençay is a great example of this kind of rind treatment. These wrinkly, flat-topped pyramids of goat's milk cheese are sprinkled with a fine layer of food-grade vegetable ash before they are aged. The alkaline ash coating lowers the cheese's pH, which helps the rind to grow on the surface of the cheese.

WAX

Cheese wax is used to protect certain varieties of cheese from moisture loss and unwanted microbes. Some waxed cheeses have come to be known by their colorful coatings, such as red-wax Gouda or Cabot Creamery's three- and five-year cheddars, which are encased in shiny black wax—almost like a sharp tuxedo jacket.

CLOTH

Large wheels that will age for several months, especially English cheddars, may be bandaged, or wrapped in cloth. First, the cheesemaker *lards* the exterior, applying a layer of fat to hold in moisture, then wraps the cheese tightly in thin muslin. This allows molds to grow on the cloth, rather than directly on the rind, and also attracts cheese mites that further develop flavor. The finished cheese has a rustic-looking surface once the cloth is removed.

FLOWERS AND HERBS

Some cheeses get an edible botanical coat during the aging process. Pressing flowers and/or herbs onto the cheese surface imparts flavor and helps with rind formation. Plus, it creates a beautiful presentation when you're ready to dig into a wedge. Fleur du Maquis, a Corsican sheep's milk cheese, is pressed with a robust mixture of dried rosemary, fennel seeds, juniper berries, and bird's eye chilis. A colorful coating of marigold, cornflower, lavender, chervil, and rose petals beautifies and brings out the sweetness in beefy, nutty Alp Blossom, made in Western Austria's hay belt.

LEAVES

Other cheeses get bundled in inedible fig, walnut, maple, cherry, or grape leaves before they age. Like other rind treatments, leaves protect the cheese, but they can also create unique flavors.

The leaves are blanched and often marinated in alcohol before being applied to cheeses. Banon, an ancient French goat's cheese, gets its soft texture and mushroomy, earthy flavors from the tannins present in its wrapper of chestnut leaves. Fruity, sweet-savory Rogue River Blue, made in Oregon, is swaddled in biodynamic Syrah grape leaves that have been macerated in pear brandy.

BARK

Some of the most sought-after European cheeses are washed-rind rounds that get so soft when ripe that they need a little support—so cheesemakers began wrapping them in flexible strips of tree bark, typically spruce, that also impart smoky, woodsy, or resin flavors. This practice has been traced back to at least the thirteenth century in the Alps and is a great example of how seasonality plays a role in cheesemaking. Lower wintertime milk production prompted farmers to produce smaller wheels rather than their usual big, brawny hard cheeses.

In addition, the cows were eating dry hay rather than their summertime diet of juicy, higher-moisture fresh grass. Because of this, the milk they produced contained a higher percentage of protein and fat, and the resulting cheeses tended to get oozy and ripe more quickly than usual, so the makers wrapped the wheels in a scaffolding of spruce bark. This kept the wheels intact, allowing for longer aging, more microbial growth, and further breakdown of the proteins in the wheel.

The result? You can dip into these cheeses from the top with bread, crackers, or a spoon to get to the luscious, scoopable, spreadable paste. Vacherin Mont d'Or is a classic bark-wrapped Alpine style. Excellent U.S. examples are Winnimere and Harbison cheeses from Jasper Hill Farm in Vermont and Merry Goat Round Spruce Reserve, a goat's milk version from Maryland's Firefly Farm.

MICROBES, BRINES, AND WASHES

The microbes cultivated on the rinds of some cheeses affect the paste within. To make a Camembert-style bloomy-rind cheese (see page 52), the cheesemaker will add *Penicillium camemberti* (makes sense, right?), which is responsible for that cheese's downy white coating. *P. camemberti* can work in tandem with other microbes, too. If you've ever seen a bloomy cheese with a wrinkly, brainlike rind, know that the yeast *Geotrichum candidum* made it happen. Another notable bacterium is *Brevibacterium linens*, which is responsible for the peachy-pink hue on some washed-rind cheeses, as well as their signature whiffy locker-room-like aromas. To create a good environment for *B. linens* and a bad one for unwanted microbes, the cheesemaker will rub or bathe the cheese in brine periodically as it ages.

Washing rinds also offers cheesemakers the chance to get creative and collaborate with craft producers of beverages like beer, cider, wine, and liquor—kindred spirits in the fermentation world—and even coffee. The addition of a little alcohol to a brine can impart unique flavors and aromas to the rind and makes a cheese perfect for pairing with the same beverage once it's ripe.

SHOULD YOU EAT THE RIND?

Short answer: yes, most of the time. Unless a cheese is covered in wax or its exterior is hard and unchewable, the rind is meant to be eaten. (And if you're dealing with a super-long-aged wheel like Parmigiano-Reggiano, save those rinds in your freezer to make an amazing umami-rich broth.) Inedible rind treatments like leaves, bark, or cloth should be discarded.

As we discussed earlier, the cheesemaker went to a lot of trouble to create a beautiful, consistent rind that protects and adds flavor and texture to the cheese. Avoiding the rind is sort of like looking at a painting by a great artist through a keyhole: you're not getting the whole picture. Nor are you getting the most bang for your buck—you paid good money for that rind you're leaving on the plate.

By at least tasting the rind of each new cheese, you're broadening your tastes and educating yourself about that cheese, its style, and its maker. Of course, if you really don't like it, you don't have to eat it—because ultimately, eating cheese should be a pleasurable sensory experience.

TYPES OF CHEESE

Despite having the same four basic ingredients, factors like seasonal milk components, types of microbes and rennet used, moisture, *affinage* techniques, and aging time mean that there are infinite possibilities in cheesemaking.

Forces like culture, geography, and economics have shaped cheesemaking around the world throughout human history, resulting in the plethora of varieties we know and love today. Still, most cheeses are typically classified into the following nine broad categories, whether because of specific techniques and recipes used to produce them or shared characteristics like flavor, texture, and appearance when they're finished.

FRESH	BRINED	BLOOMY RIND
ALPINE	CHEDDAR	GOUDA
BLUE	PASTA FILATA	WASHED RIND

In addition to these categories, there are some other general ways to classify cheese. We'll look at those in the chapters ahead.

FRESH CHEESES

These high-moisture, unripened cheeses are typically sold within a few days—or hours—of being made. They are usually soft, spreadable, or spoonable, although some are pressed until dry and crumbly or stretched into tender balls or braids.

Because of their relatively high moisture content, fresh cheeses have a shorter shelf life than other varieties—typically a week or so—so don't forget about them in your cheese drawer for long. Your nose will tell you if they've gone off. An unpleasant spoiled-milk odor means it's got to go, whereas a pleasantly lactic or tangy scent indicates a fresh cheese that's still good for eating.

VARIETIES TO TRY

Chèvre: The tangy, spreadable, rindless version of this fresh goat's milk cheese is most commonly seen outside France, where the name can also be used to describe longer-aged young goat cheeses that develop a rind and more complex, concentrated flavors. Similar cheeses made in this style are *fromage blanc*, made with cow's milk, and *brebis*, made with sheep's milk.

Ricotta: This spoonable, grainy cheese is made from the whey left over from the production of cheeses like Parmigiano-Reggiano and mozzarella. The liquid is cooked and acid is added to capture the remaining whey protein. Ricotta salata, a firm, grateable version, is pressed, salted, and aged for at least three months to preserve the cheese and develop its flavor.

Paneer: In northern India and Pakistan, this fresh cheese is made by just barely boiling milk, coagulating with lemon juice or vinegar, and then draining the curds. Because it doesn't have much flavor on its own, paneer is typically drained and used to make sweets, or pressed until firm and either fried or added to saucy, savory dishes like *saag paneer*. (See page 136 for how to make your own paneer at home.)

Queso fresco: Just one of the many fresh cheeses produced in Mexico, *queso fresco* literally means "fresh cheese." The acidified curds of this variety are drained and pressed into milky rounds. It has a delicate flavor and can be sliced and fried in oil or crumbled fresh over enchiladas, tacos, or *elotes*.

BRINED CHEESES

The wheels of these cheeses may be stored in a solution of salt and a little calcium or dry-salted. The longer a cheese is aged in brine, the sharper its flavor.

VARIETIES TO TRY

Feta: This soft, crumbly Greek cheese is typically made with goat's or sheep's milk. Tangy and salt-forward yet creamy and lactic, it's used for everything from filling flaky pastries to stuffing eggplants.

Domiati: This Egyptian cheese—which dates back at least 2,500 years—is unique in that salt is added directly to the milk before the curds form. After draining and pressing, the wheels can be eaten fresh or aged in brine for three to four months, resulting in a squeaky, salty cheese.

Halloumi: Originating on the island of Cyprus, halloumi is used throughout the Mediterranean and Middle East. With its very high melting point, it will keep its shape and develop a crisp golden-brown crust and tender, squeaky interior when fried or grilled.

BLOOMY RINDS

Also known as soft-ripened cheeses, this category includes some of the world's most exalted wheels. Textures can be lush and oozy or cloudlike and chalky, and flavor notes run the gamut: milk, butter, mushrooms, beef broth, barnyard, etc.

Bloomy-rind cheeses may be eaten young, when the paste is solid, or they may be aged for several weeks to develop a cream line—a layer of gooey richness between the rind and the paste. This luscious feature is the result of those lively microbes on the rind breaking down the proteins and fats in the paste beneath.

There are two subgroups of bloomy rinds. The first is made with rennet as the coagulant and has a stronger interior structure thanks to the enzymes and the calcium they help retain; this gives the cheese more elasticity. Think Brie- and Camembert-style cheeses, with a texture that's dense and buttery and a tendency toward stronger, savory flavors.

The other subgroup is the lactic bloomies, in which a combination of acid and heat is primarily responsible for coagulating the milk; little or no rennet is used. Because of this, coagulation takes a lot longer than with rennet-set bloomies and requires more lactic acid to be produced during the process. This results in a paste with a chalky or cloudlike texture (because acid dissolves calcium) and flavor profiles ranging from bright and citrusy to milky and earthy. The lactic bloomy style is exemplified by traditional goat cheeses of France's Loire Valley.

As you explore the world of bloomy-rind cheeses, you'll see the terms *double crème* and *triple crème*. These indicate that cream was added to the milk before culturing. Double-crème cheeses contain 60% to 75% butterfat, and triple-crème wheels must be at least 75% butterfat. Bloomies that do not have additional cream are typically around 45% butterfat.

RENNET-SET BLOOMIES TO TRY

Brie de Meaux: This large-format cow's milk wheel with a supple paste and nutty, earthy notes is France's premiere bloomy cheese, named for the region (Brie) and town (Meaux) where it's produced. Get your hands on raw wheels (the real stuff) if you can; versions imported to the U.S. are pasteurized.

Brebirousse d'Argental: With its high fat content, sheep's milk lends itself wonderfully to bloomy-style cheeses. Gooey and silky in texture with big savory flavors, this French style gets its bright-orange coat from annatto, the same seed used to color blocks of cheddar.

Saint-André: If finding artisanal wheels is a challenge where you live, set your sights on a wedge of this rich triple-crème cow's milk beauty, which is available in many grocery stores and supermarkets but is still produced on French farms rather than in factories. Cut its creaminess and play up its tangy sour-cream notes with a glass of bone-dry bubbly.

LACTIC BLOOMIES TO TRY

Valençay: With a mottled gray color thanks to bloomy white mold and a vegetable ash coating, plus the *Geotrichum* crags on its rind, this truncated pyramid resembles a snow-capped mountain. At a few weeks, the cheese is young and milky; as it ages, it develops an earthy forest-floor quality.

Crottin de Chavignol: This little round goat's milk cheese from Sancerre is named for its similar size and shape to *crottin*—that is, manure. Covered in white or blue mold, this cheese can be enjoyed young and firm or mature, funky, and mushroomy.

Coupole: Vermont Creamery's award-winning goat's milk snowball has a brainy, coral-like edible rind enclosing a sweet, grassy, velvety paste. It's lovely with a glass of Riesling or fruity lambic.

PICKING BLOOMIES: WHAT TO LOOK FOR WHEN YOU SHOP

When shopping for bloomy-rind cheeses, it's worth it to spring for the good stuff. Avoid precut plastic-wrapped wedges; they tend to be bland and rubbery. Buy cut-to-order wedges or small-format whole wheels if possible.

The texture of a ripe bloomy can range from firm yet squeezable to water balloon, depending on the cheese, the purveyor, and consumer preference (you're more likely to encounter advanced-age bloomies in France, where funkier flavors and textures are prized, than in North America). The latter will be *very* ripe and should be eaten within a day or two at most. If, once you get your bloomy home, you notice a sticky, cracked, or completely brown rind, colorful molds, or a very firm texture, take it back and ask for a replacement or refund. It's past its prime and hasn't been cared for properly.

If you smell a powerful whiff of ammonia, remove the cheese from its packaging and air it out on the counter for an hour or two. This may take care of the problem, which is caused by an overproduction of ammonia by microbes during the aging process (an issue that affects bloomy- and washed-rind cheeses in particular). If it still smells like your cat's litter box, it's time to return it to your monger and alert them to the issue.

ALPINE CHEESES

Named for the mountains of France, Switzerland, and Italy where they're made, Alpine cheeses developed thanks to a farming practice known as *transhumance*. As snow melted in spring, shepherds would bring their cows up the mountains to graze on high-altitude pastures; in fall, they'd head back down to the valleys.

As they followed the wildflower-rich mountain meadows, farmers pooled their herds together to get a higher volume of milk. They also built chalets—cheesemaking huts—along their routes where these large, long-aged wheels of cheese could be produced as needed during the seasonal journey.

We might think of fondue as a cheesy (heh) 1970s throwback, but the practice originated with eighteenth-century Swiss peasants looking for a way to make hard Alpine cheeses and stale bread more palatable. The Alpine tradition also gave us raclette (see page 122).

VARIETIES TO TRY

Emmental: These massive—as in 220-pound—wheels of nutty, fruity raw cow's milk cheese are aged for three to six months. This is the real deal that American "Swiss" cheese is trying to be, complete with signature walnut-sized eyes in the paste.

Gruyère: The name describes both a protected Swiss cheese and a wider category of name-protected mountain cheeses that includes Beaufort and Comté from France and Asiago and Montasio from Italy. Flavors range from walnuts to celery to brown butter to toffee.

Fontina Val d'Aosta: Known for its meltability, this pungent protected cheese made in the mountains of northwestern Italy is a far cry from the bland, flabby knockoffs you may have tried.

Some important firm and semifirm cheeses don't fit into the categories here and on pages 58–60. These cheeses can be categorized based on how moisture is removed from the curds and young wheels; experts tend to think of them as either cheeses that are uncooked (without heat applied to the curds) and pressed—like Gouda, Manchego, Monterey Jack, and milled-curd cheeses like cheddar and Cantal—or cooked and pressed cheeses, such as Pecorino. This distinction explains why some of these common styles don't fit into the broad geographic families on the following pages.

CHEDDARS

Cheddar might seem like the quintessential American cheese—after all, the U.S. produces more than three billion pounds of this firm, aged cheese each year. But in fact, it originated in . . . Cheddar, a village in southwest England, nine hundred or so years ago.

This style of cheese can be sold after just a few months or aged for many years. It may be deep golden yellow, white, or dyed bright orange; it's produced in huge 40-pound blocks or little wax-dipped truckles the size of hockey pucks. Its texture ranges from pliant and meltable to dry and crumbly, with flavors that are bright and sharp or nutty, fruity, or toasty. Traditional English-style farmhouse cheddars tend to be drier, with a muskier flavor, whereas U.S. cheddars are usually sweeter and higher in moisture. Great examples of both styles exist (see below).

Cheddar isn't just a noun—it's also a verb describing the way this cheese is produced. The curds are pressed together and cut into slabs, which are continually turned and stacked on top of one another, releasing moisture and increasing acidity. After cheddaring is complete, the curds are milled into tiny pieces and salted, then formed into wheels and pressed. The curds can also be sold fresh. You can tell real, fresh cheddar curds by their bouncy texture and signature squeak when you bite into them.

VARIETIES TO TRY

Montgomery's Cheddar: Along with Keene's and Westcombe Dairy, Montgomery's bandaged raw-milk drums are among the top English-style farmhouse cheddars in the world. Aged for 12 to 18 months, these wheels feature a golden straw-colored paste with deeply savory flavor ranging from nutty to meaty.

Prairie Breeze: Blocks of this sweeter, white, pasteurized cow's milk cheddar are aged for at least nine months at Iowa's Milton Creamery. Crunchy cheese lovers, take note: its crumbly yet creamy texture is shot through with delectable calcium crystals.

Cabot Cheddar: The farmer-owned Cabot cooperative in Vermont is responsible for some of the best cheddar in the world. Fruity, tangy Cabot Clothbound—a raw cow's milk collaboration with the expert *affineurs* at the Cellars at Jasper Hill—is a must-try, as are its high-quality blocks for everyday eating. Cabot's Extra-Sharp Vermont Cheddar is a constant presence in my fridge.

GOUDAS

Synonymous with the Netherlands since its signature technique of washing, cooking, and stirring the curds was perfected by cheesemakers there in the seventeenth century, Gouda is named for a Dutch town that's home to one of Europe's largest cheese markets.

The curd-washing process makes for a sweeter finished product, giving young wheels a mild, milky flavor and supple texture; varieties aged for a year or more have a toffee-like, caramelized quality. Although there are some outliers, generally the best Goudas are made in Holland.

VARIETIES TO TRY

Prima Donna: Combining Parmesan cultures with a Gouda-style make, this long-aged Dutch cheese is increasingly easy to find in supermarkets.

Midnight Moon: Produced in Holland for California's Cypress Grove, this cheese has notes of brown butter and caramel. It may convert the goat-averse.

Seven Sisters: The small herd of Jersey cows at the Farm at Doe Run in Pennsylvania makes this Alpine-Gouda cross sweet, nutty, and herbaceous.

BLUE CHEESES

Cheeses in the blue mold family bring big flavors ranging from spicy to toasty to sour to chocolatey. Some cheese lovers crave this style's signature pungency, whereas others just can't stomach it.

Blue cheeses get their namesake hue from two different cultures: *Penicillium roqueforti* and *Penicillium glaucum*, part of the genus of molds from which penicillin is derived. The former creates a vivid greenish-blue mold and a more aggressive flavor profile—think Roquefort, obviously. By contrast, the latter produces a milder dessert-like blue.

A common misconception is that the colorful stripes of mold you see on a cut wedge of blue-veined cheese are injected into the wheels. In fact, the culture is added to the liquid milk, but the mold can only grow in the presence of oxygen, so the wheel must be pierced with a long needle. Some blue cheeses such as Monte Enebro, a goat's-milk round, have blue mold applied only to their rinds, not inoculated into the milk. This gives the spicy rind and the lactic paste contrasting flavors.

VARIETIES TO TRY

Roquefort: Only seven producers make true Roquefort: an intense, complex, and ancient blue made exclusively from the raw milk of Laucaune sheep. Rindless wheels of this spicy, buttery, tangy AOC-protected cheese are aged in underground limestone caves in the South of France. Pair it with stone fruits, honey, and walnuts or a glass of Sauternes.

Colston Bassett Stilton: Colston Bassett is the rare producer making Stilton with preindustrial methods, hand-ladling curds rather than producing wheels in factories. The result is a rich, fudgy blue that melts on the tongue. Because this pasteurized cow's milk wheel is pierced less than other blues—meaning less mold growth—its flavor is sweeter.

Rogue River Blue: The blue cheese experts—they make seven different kinds—at Oregon's Rogue Creamery triumphed with this cheese at the 2019 World Cheese Awards. Made only with luscious fall milk and aged wrapped in grape leaves soaked in pear liqueur, it's a seasonal treat that's worth its steeper-than-most price tag.

HATE BLUE CHEESE?
TRY A GATEWAY BLUE

Not into the piquant, tongue-popping qualities of blue cheese? I encourage the blue-averse to try again with such milder, friendlier "gateway blues" as Bleu d'Auvergne that are cultured with *P. glaucum*, which creates those sweeter, nutty, chocolatey notes. You can also ask your friendly neighborhood cheesemonger to try a nibble of the most accessible blue in their case.

If you're shopping at the supermarket, Cambozola—a hybrid of Camembert and Gorgonzola—has the lush texture and buttery flavors of a ripe bloomy with only intermittent blue mold. It's also pretty affordable, so if after tasting it you're still not convinced, your pocketbook will take less of a hit when you give it away to a blue-loving friend.

PASTA FILATA CHEESES

Did you know that milky, tender fresh mozzarella (*fior di latte*) and sharp, firm provolone are in the same family of cheeses? The Italian words *pasta filata* translate to "spun paste," referring to the way these cheeses are stretched or pulled. This category includes string cheeses like Oaxaca, Armenian string cheese, and the plastic-wrapped snack sticks in your kid's lunch box, too.

The signature smooth texture of pasta filata cheeses results from very hot water being added to the curds after the whey is drained. This melts the curds together so that they can be gently manipulated into a silky, supple mass and stretched. The fresh cheese is shaped into logs, balls, or braids. Aged cheeses are brined and tied into shapes ranging from melons to pears to flasks (imagine a teardrop-shaped bottle with a string around its neck) and hung to dry for anywhere from a few months to more than a year.

VARIETIES TO TRY

Mozzarella: We're not talking about the rubbery shreds that go on pizza, but rather soft, tender fresh mozzarella—sometimes called *fior di latte* when made with cow's milk and *mozzarella di bufala* when made with water buffalo milk. You can find it wrapped in plastic or stored in brine at cheese shops, gourmet markets, and Italian grocers. Or order up a batch of frozen mozzarella curd from Pennsylvania-based Caputo Brothers Creamery, defrost it in your fridge, and stretch it yourself to get the freshest mozz possible.

Queso Oaxaca: Also known as *quesillo de hebra*, Mexico's sole pasta filata cheese is stretched into long strings, then twisted into a ball like yarn. Tangy and lactic, it is ideally eaten fresh and works as a beautiful melter in quesadillas. Traditionally, it is made with raw milk, but most versions produced on a large scale or outside Mexico are pasteurized.

Suffolk Punch: One of the handmade natural cheeses (see page 70) produced by Vermont's Parish Hill Creamery, this raw cow's milk cheese gets its signature gourd shape from the traditional practice of tying two cheeses to either end of a rope and carrying them on horseback, saddlebag style. It's smooth and buttery at three months; drier and peppery at six.

WASHED-RIND CHEESES

People will say that a particularly odoriferous cheese smells like sweaty feet or a hamper of dirty laundry. Usually, they're referring to cheeses in this group.

These cheeses are bathed, soaked, or rubbed with a salt brine to promote the growth of pungent microbes. Younger, softer wheels typically have a tacky peachy-pink rind. The russet hue—called *morge*—on the rinds of longer-aged cheeses like Gruyère is subtler.

VARIETIES TO TRY

Taleggio: This PDO stinker made with raw or pasteurized cow's milk is square, its striated rind streaked with pink, red, and green molds. The paste beneath its funky, gritty rind is soft, supple, and herbaceous.

Époisses: This lush, brandy-washed lactic cheese is so ripe and creamy it comes packaged in a wood box—so you can dip a hunk of baguette or plunge in with a spoon.

Rush Creek Reserve: This bark-wrapped beauty by Wisconsin's Uplands Creamery is produced only with extra-rich fall and winter cow's milk. Sub it for the raw-milk Vacherin Mont d'Or, which can't be had in the States.

SMOKED AND FLAVORED CHEESES

Smoked cheeses get their flavor from the rind out. Some wheels are cold smoked—exposed directly to wood smoke at a low temperature—which often imparts the best flavor and helps preserve the cheese. Other times, liquid smoke is brushed onto the cheese's exterior. Both can bring out savory, sweet, or umami flavors.

Flavored cheeses typically get an extra kick from mix-ins like dried herbs and spices added to the curds after the whey has been drained off. Flavors can include anything from black peppercorn to saffron to dried apricots.

Another way to flavor and preserve younger cheeses is to marinate them in oil with dried herbs, spices, or red pepper flakes. This is frequently done with fresher or brined cheeses like chèvre, labneh, feta, and mozzarella.

Beer-curd cheese is also (sort of) a flavored cheese. After the curds are cut, the cheesemaker drains away a portion of the whey and replaces it with flavorful beer. The curds soak up that flavor, and then the cheese is drained and hooped as usual. What results is a cheese that captures and transforms the character of the beer.

PROCESSED CHEESE AND PROCESS CHEESE FOODS

Cheese is an expression of a maker's craftsmanship and a region's unique terroir as much as it is a food product. Nevertheless, much of the cheese we eat is produced on a massive industrial scale. Commodity production results in cheeses that are all the same, made from the milk of thousands of cows that has been mixed together.

This is the shredded mozzarella and shaker parmesan on your pizza, the Swiss on your ham sandwich, the big blocks of orange cheddar at the supermarket. Though there's nothing wrong with these cheeses—aside from their connection to an environmentally and economically exploitative industrialized food system—they typically offer more in terms of affordability and accessibility rather than quality, craftsmanship, or provenance.

Foods such as Velveeta, Cheez Whiz, and Dorito dust take the desire for durability and longevity to an extreme. They're so processed that, in the United States, they don't even meet the legal definition of cheese; that's why their labels bear the terms *pasteurized process cheese food* or *pasteurized process cheese* rather than simply *cheese*. Real cheese is an ingredient in process cheese; it's shredded and combined with oil, water, salt, coloring, preservatives, and fillers (no wonder it can't legally be called cheese). The mixture is agitated and heated, and then emulsifying salts are added to dissolve the cheese's calcium structure and allow protein, fat, and water to blend together. The result is a homogenous, long-lasting product that melts beautifully without breaking—but stretches the definition of cheese past the breaking point.

There are plenty of cheese lovers who wouldn't be caught dead with a package of Kraft singles in their refrigerator. At the same time, these long-lasting cheeses are some of the most affordable and accessible for many households (and truthfully, they can taste pretty damn good). To me, processed cheeses and commodity cheeses have their place. It might not necessarily be on a cheese board, but processed cheese singles melt on a burger like no other. Sometimes, you're just craving a slice from your neighborhood pizza joint topped with a heavy dusting of powdered parmesan. It's up to you, the consumer, to decide what you want to spend your dollars on.

NATURAL CHEESES

On the other end of the spectrum are cheeses that seek to bring back bygone cheesemaking techniques in order to highlight livelier flavors and American terroir.

You've probably heard of natural wines, which are made with some combination of organic growing practices in the field and minimal intervention during the winemaking process. These methods allow for bigger, unconventional, and/or particularly unique flavors expressing the terroir of where the wine was produced.

In cheesemaking, *natural* cheese—for lack of a better term—is made with the traditional methods used throughout most of human history: raising cows on pasture, making cheese with raw milk, using native cultures, making your own rennet, sourcing salt locally, letting natural rinds grow. Few commercial-scale producers, even in Europe, practice cheesemaking this way anymore. But adopting some or all of these methods is an excellent way to make fantastic, utterly singular cheeses that truly capture a taste of place.

In the U.S., many artisan cheesemakers follow most of these traditional practices. But only one, Parish Hill Creamery in southwest Vermont, employs all of them. Cheesemakers and owners Peter Dixon and Rachel Fritz Schall make big, flavorful Alpine-style cheeses. To develop their recipes, Dixon, a dairy consultant, put his research on traditional cheesemaking techniques into practice. He and Schall use raw milk from nearby Elm Lea Farm collected only during summer months when the cows are grazing on fresh grass, make their own rennet, source sea salt from Maine, and cultivate native cultures. The results are richly aromatic full-flavored cheeses unlike any others—because their characteristics are so tightly tied to the place where they're made.

DOMESTIC ARTISAN CHEESES

Before North America was colonized by Europeans, dairy wasn't a thing in the New World. In what would become the U.S., British colonizers introduced dairy animals along with their cheesemaking traditions, which at the time were highly regional, meaning that no two farms made exactly the same version of a style of cheese. Early Americans then did the same.

But during the nineteenth and early twentieth centuries, the Industrial Revolution consolidated and commodified cheesemaking and dairy farming. Hundreds of regional styles in the U.S. and U.K. were lost as dairy farmers sought efficiency by pooling milk together, moving production to factories, and developing standardized recipes that prioritized shelf stability and portability rather than flavor or character. This trend continued through the American postwar period, when agriculture consolidated and industrialized pretty much across the board.

Starting in the 1970s and 1980s, a group of (mostly women) would-be farmers, inspired by the back-to-the-land ethos of the cultural revolution, turned to an agrarian lifestyle—and some of them began making cheese. Their efforts helped foster a growing consumer interest in farm-to-table eating and local foods, which intensified in the early 2000s and continues to today. This prompted an explosion in artisan cheesemaking. Although many of these U.S. makers took inspiration from European classics, their passion for experimentation coupled with unique terroir meant that there are now hundreds of distinctive and exciting award-winning artisan cheeses made in the U.S.

A quick Google search or visit to your local farmers market will help you find makers near you. One of the most rewarding experiences as a cheese lover is supporting a producer making great cheese in your own community or region.

In addition to the many domestic offerings mentioned in the preceding pages, turn the page for just a few of the many excellent American-made cheeses and producers to try.

CHEESE	MAKER	STATE
Beecher's Cheddar	Beecher's Handmade Cheese	Washington
Wabash Cannonball	Capriole	Indiana
Tiger Lily	Tulip Tree Creamery	Indiana
Havilah	Cherry Grove Farm	New Jersey
Finger Lakes Gold	Lively Run Dairy	New York
Dutch Knuckle	Sugar House Creamery	New York
Birchrun Blue	Birchrun Hills Farm	Pennsylvania
Grayson	Meadow Creek Dairy	Virginia
Verano	Vermont Shepherd	Vermont
Moses Sleeper	The Cellars at Jasper Hill	Vermont
Farmhouse Cave-Aged	Orb Weaver Creamery	Vermont
Pleasant Ridge Reserve	Uplands Creamery	Wisconsin
Point Reyes Blue	Point Reyes Creamery	California

CHEESE GEOGRAPHY

You may have noticed that most of the cheeses in the preceding pages are produced in the Americas, Europe, or Western Asia. Cultured dairy products have a history just about everywhere dairy animals are raised, from paneer in India to yak's milk cheese in Tibet to yogurt-like *ikiguvuto*, an indigenous fermented drink made from cow's milk in Rwanda, and today, they're imported and exported around the globe.

Dairying and cheesemaking originated in the Fertile Crescent thousands of years ago and spread through Europe, where climate and geography lent themselves to raising dairy animals and making and aging cheese from their milk as an essential food source. As Europeans colonized much of the world, they brought dairy animals and cheesemaking practices with them.

Western cultural hegemony, as well as deep history, strong government support, and cultural identification with traditional cheeses in European countries, means that Europe's cheeses are widely considered the best in the world. However, cheesemakers in places not traditionally associated with cheese are staking their claim. The next step is getting these exciting new cheeses into the hands of cheese lovers around the world.

South Africa: The nation has a long dairy history and cheese culture due to colonization by the Dutch and English, but twentieth-century regulations stymied dairy farmers' ability to produce cheese using their own milk. Today, artisan cheesemakers produce award-winning takes on European-style cheeses with South African identity, such as Huguenot, a brawny, nutty natural-rind wheel from Dalewood Fromage, and Kilembe, a hard aged goat's milk offering from Belnori Boutique Cheesery.

Japan: European-style cheeses have been produced on a large scale in Japan since the early twentieth century, but it's only since the 1980s that the country's small-scale artisan cheese community has come into its own. At Fromagerie Sen, outside Tokyo, owner and microbiologist Chayo Shibata cultivates native cultures for her recipes. Cheesemaker Nozomu Miyajima of Hokkaido's Kyodogakusha Shintoku Farm has won global awards for Sakura, a delicate bloomy round wrapped in a shiso leaf and topped with a pickled cherry blossom.

Barbados: Hatchman's Cheese owner Andrea Power wanted to create diversity and sustainability in the island's dairy industry, so she started making cow's and goat's milk cheeses from a recipe her father taught her when she was a child. Power sources local cow's and goat's milk to produce her Caribbean takes on European-style cheeses, from Jack cheese spiced with Scotch bonnet pepper to chèvre spiked with bright, tangy sorrel.

China: The Chinese artisan cheese movement is in its infancy but on the rise. Leading the way is Liu Yang, cheesemaker and proprietor of Le Fromager de Pekin, outside Beijing. Yang, who trained for years in France before returning home to share his love of cheese, makes French-style cheeses like the Camembert-esque Beijing Gray.

WHY SOME CHEESES MELT DIFFERENTLY

You may have noticed that macaroni and cheese recipes often call for two cheeses: one sharper, more flavorful cheese and one that's softer and milder. We do the same with pizza, counting on easy melters like mozzarella to get stretchy and bubbly in the oven before showering umami-rich parm on top.

Why is that? Because not all cheeses melt alike.

The structure of cheese is mostly protein. Calcium is like the scaffolding holding protein, fat, and water in place. In general, cheeses higher in fat and moisture will melt more easily—think young Gouda, mild cheddar, and mozzarella. Cheeses with lower moisture, like Pecorino or Parmigiano-Reggiano, won't melt as well. If it's oozy, hot cheese sauce with lots of flavor that you crave, blend the two to get the best of both worlds.

There's another factor at play: acid, which breaks down that calcium scaffolding. Cheeses with less acid won't melt well because they have lots of calcium holding things together. Cheeses with more acid don't melt well either because all that acid holds the casein together. The upside with some low-pH cheeses is that they can be fried or grilled and still keep their shape.

Halloumi is probably the best known of this type, but there are others that can take the heat: Leipäjuusto, also known as Finnish "bread cheese," is cooked until browned after it's pressed. Another is paneer, known for keeping its cube shape in a bubbling pot of spiced pureed greens. (See page 136 for how to make paneer at home.) These cheeses also have a tender, slightly bouncy texture and squeak when you bite into them.

In the middle of these two extremes are cheeses that have the right amounts of fat, moisture, and acidity to melt really well. Because the casein proteins have unfurled from their tightly coiled micelles during the cheesemaking process, they form long strands when stretched and pulled. The longer a cheese ages, the more likely that proteolysis—the breakdown of those protein strands—has occurred, weakening the structure of the cheese and causing it to "break." That's what happens when you try to melt cheese and you get a warm lump sitting in a puddle of fat.

So, when in doubt, go for a proven melter—mozzarella, young Gouda, Raclette, fontina, block cheddar—or blend a softer, milder cheese with a hard, flavorful one.

APPELLATION SYSTEMS

Many European cheeses have been made for hundreds or even thousands of years. To protect the traditional production methods and geographic identities of these cheeses, strongholds like France and Italy have created special requirements called designation of origin, or DOs.

Such designations require that a cheese be produced in a specific region, use raw milk from a specific breed of cow fed a certain kind of feed and/or milked during a certain season, or use a particular recipe or technique. It's illegal for the makers of a cheese or other controlled food product that doesn't meet those requirements to use that protected name. This is why we have mass-produced *parmesan* cheese in the U.S. True Parmigiano-Reggiano can only be produced in a few Italian provinces; similar products that don't meet the requirements have to be called something else.

Purchasing a cheese with a DO label lets you know that you're getting a certain level of quality and authenticity in an industry where style names are often used generically to describe non-DO cheeses, whether to intentionally mimic the real thing or simply take inspiration from a widely recognized style. It also supports the regional producers who make the effort to preserve these traditional foods.

France: Look for the Appellation of Controlled Origin (AOC) label on cheeses like Roquefort, Comté, Gruyère, and Crottin de Chavignol. Unfortunately, many are not available in the U.S. due to restrictions on raw milk, but pasteurized (non-DO) versions can be found.

Italy: Protected Designation of Origin (PDO) and Protected Geographical Indication (PGI) seals certify cheeses like Parmigiano-Reggiano, Taleggio, Asiago, Pecorino, Provolone, and Mozzarella di Bufala Campana.

Spain: Denominación de Origen (DO) cheeses include Manchego, Idiazábal, and Cabrales.

In addition to the countries above, Belgium, Greece, Germany, Austria, England, and Portugal have their own DO systems and protected cheeses.

EATING
CHEESE

HOW TO BUY CHEESE

You're probably thinking, "I know how to buy cheese. Pick up cheese, put cheese in shopping cart, exchange money for cheese."

But it's not quite so simple because cheese is a *living food*. Many of the microbes we've discussed are slowly changing the character and quality of that piece of cheese, even after it's in your fridge. Cheesemaking is basically carefully controlled decomposition.

Once you cut into a cheese, the aging process stops. But the potential for deterioration of quality, absorbing off-flavors, drying out, or growing unwanted molds increases. How your cheese is packaged—and how long it was in that package—makes a difference in the overall quality.

To get the best-quality product for your dairy dollar, purchase your cheese from a cut-to-order counter at your supermarket, independent grocer, cheese shop, or food co-op. When a cheesemonger cuts a wedge before your eyes, you're getting the freshest possible product.

Ideally, they're also wrapping it in cheese paper—which will protect it from the dry environment of your fridge while allowing it to breathe—rather than plastic wrap or unlined butcher paper. Purchasing wedges from your local cheesemaker that were cut the day before and immediately wrapped in cheese paper or plastic is another good option.

If you don't have a cut-to-order counter in your area, plastic-wrapped pieces of cheese that are precut in-house and dated are the next best thing. Basically, you don't want your cheese sitting around in plastic for days (or weeks) because the lack of breathability will negatively affect the quality. Plastic can also impart an off-flavor to the surface of the cheese due to oxidation caused by light shining through the clear packaging (which is why it's a good idea to gently scrape a knife over the cut surface of cheese packed this way before serving).

The packaging option you're most likely to see in a conventional supermarket is vacuum-sealed plastic. Although some cheeses—many block cheddars, for example—are aged this way for many months, it's the least ideal option for the same reason large-scale producers, distributors, and retailers enjoy it: because the cheese lasts a long time. However, this effectively mummifies your cheese. In addition to the surface oxidation issue, airtight plastic wrapping can trap in microbial or enzymatic by-products like ammonia and can allow undesirable microbes that produce off-flavors to thrive, which will affect the cheese's taste.

WHAT'S SO SPECIAL ABOUT CHEESE PAPER?

You already have a drawer in your kitchen full of aluminum foil, wax paper, parchment paper, and plastic wrap to protect foods and keep them fresh. Why add cheese paper to the mix?

Cheese paper is a composite material—typically an outer wax-coated paper and an inner porous layer of plastic fused together. This combination creates the ideal conditions for cheese, whether it's a little bloomy button or a cut wedge of English cheddar. The paper is structured enough to protect the cheese without suffocating it, and its opacity blocks oxidizing light. The plastic maintains humidity, releases excess moisture, and defends against the drying climate in your refrigerator. This ingenious material protects your cheese while allowing it to breathe, keeping it in the ideal condition for you to enjoy while greatly extending its shelf life.

For instructions on wrapping with cheese paper, see page 93.

MAKE FRIENDS WITH YOUR CHEESEMONGER

If your area has a grocery store, dedicated cheese shop, or farmers market stand with a well-trained cheesemonger behind the counter, you're lucky! Here's how to build a friendly relationship that will mean many happy years of cheese snacks and knowledge for you and better business for them.

Don't be shy. It's easy to feel awkward or intimidated talking to sales staff when you're shopping. But your cheesemonger is there to make your purchasing experience as pleasant and rewarding as possible. It's only fair that you hold up your end of the bargain by respectfully taking them up on it.

Be prepared. A good monger will have a ready answer to common questions like "What's good right now?" or "What's your favorite?" and be able to guide you to a tasty selection. But it helps to provide info up-front: Are you looking for a great fondue blend? Sourcing cheeses for a small dinner party or a big New Year's Eve bash? Are you about to take some souvenir wedges on a five-hour plane ride? Let them know so they can take these details into account.

Don't be a sample hog. Samples exist for one reason only: to entice you into buying cheese. If you swing by the sampling tray and grab a cube without buying, that's not a big deal. But if you're gnawing through an array of cheeses with no intention of purchasing, you're wasting your monger's valuable time and energy.

Know the minimum. Most cheese shops won't sell pieces smaller than a quarter pound, so keep that in mind if you're browsing on a tight budget or shopping for educational purposes. Looking to try a bunch of different types without spending a lot? Many cheese shops keep a basket of odd pieces that cost only a few dollars each.

Keep records. If you're serious about cheese education, track what you've tasted. Many cheese shops sell cute notebooks for exactly this purpose, but you can keep notes on your phone or even take a picture of each cheese with its label to help you keep track. Some cheese shops keep a record of regular customers' purchases, so that you're never disappointed when you can't find a fondly remembered wedge whose name escapes you.

WHICH CHEESES SHOULD YOU BUY?

Whether you're hitting up a cheese shop or your neighborhood grocer, a few simple guidelines will help you select a great mix of wedges.

Choose contrasting cheeses. This rule can be applied in so many ways. Pick a cow's, sheep's, and goat's milk cheese made in different styles. Choose a soft, a medium-soft or semifirm, and a hard cheese. Or use color as your guide: a bloomy rind with a snowy white paste, a hay-colored aged tomme with a mottled gray rind, and a sticky peachy-pink washed rind.

Choose similar cheeses. Try a handful of different styles from the same maker. Manchegos at different ages. All ash-rubbed cheeses, or all blues, or all goat cheeses. This approach can show off the diversity of options in a single style, milk type, or region. Serve pieces with contrasting profiles on the same platter or board.

Go regional. This can be as general as "domestic" or as specific as "local" or "Iberian Peninsula." Look for cheeses that exemplify that region while providing contrast.

There are a ton of other themes you can build around cheeses: Cheeses with flowers on the rind. Cheeses enrobed in black wax, Dracula's cape style, for Halloween, plus some bright orange wheels to play up the theme. Cheeses with herbs added. Cheeses made with beer. Leaf-wrapped cheeses. All the cheddars of the rainbow. You get the idea.

HOW MUCH CHEESE SHOULD YOU BUY?

Budget for 1–2 ounces per person *per cheese* for a dinner party. Plan for 2 ounces if you're serving cheese early in the evening, because your guests are likelier to eat more before a meal. If you're serving cheese as dessert, shoot closer to 1 ounce of each per person. If cheese is the main event, plan on 8 ounces of cheese per person overall, plus charcuterie, bread, and accoutrements.

HOW TO STORE CHEESE

Once you get your cheese home, it's important to care for it properly. If your refrigerator has a cheese drawer, now is a great time to use it. This drawer exists to protect cheese from spills, smells, and drying out in the cold air. You can also store cheese in the butter compartment on the door or in the crisper, as long as it's dry.

If all the special compartments and drawers in your fridge are already occupied, never fear. You can create the effect of a cheese drawer with a plastic food storage container with a lid. Just pop your cheeses in and put the lid on, but leave it slightly open rather than sealing it all the way to allow for airflow.

So, how long will these carefully protected cheeses last? The sooner you can eat your cheese after bringing it home, the better—but you do have some leeway, depending on what you bought:

- Fresh cheeses like *fromage blanc* typically keep for only a week in a fridge before they start to get funky (and not in a good way).

- Fresh mozzarella packed in water should be eaten as soon as possible, but you can push it to five days.

- For a small round of soft-ripened cheese that hasn't been cut, a younger, firmer wheel can hang out in the fridge for one to two weeks, whereas a super-soft ultra-ripe wheel should be eaten immediately.

- As long as they're well wrapped and refrigerated, semifirm and firm cheeses can be stored for two weeks; hard cheeses like Parmigiano-Reggiano, long-aged Gouda, or other grateable wheels can last for three weeks. You may have to scrape or trim off a little surface mold, but the paste should still be safe to eat, if not quite as delicious as the day you brought it home.

To be absolutely sure, ask your monger for advice when buying.

HOW TO WRAP CHEESE

If you're able to open the little cheese present your monger wrapped for you without tearing the paper, following their folds is a great way to rewrap a hunk you've only partially eaten. But try your own hand at it, too. Wrapping wedges from start to finish is an important skill for any cheese lover to learn.

If your wrapping looks crooked, wrinkled, or otherwise wonky the first few times, don't worry—as long as the cheese paper is tightly covering the cheese surface with no portions exposed to the air, you're doing it right! Crisp corners and symmetry will come with practice.

WRAPPING A WEDGE OF HARD CHEESE

Hard wedges are the simplest to wrap. Place the wedge on a sheet of cheese paper with one cut side up, the fat end pointed toward a corner, and the skinny end pointing to the middle of the paper. Fold the corner snugly over the fat end. Crease the edges of this fold tightly against the rind on either side to cleanly hide the excess.

Next, fold an adjacent corner tightly over the top of the wedge, taking care to overlap the first fold. Repeat with the opposite corner. Your wedge should now be swaddled with extra paper sticking out on the skinny end. Tuck in errant corners, then fold the excess paper over the top of the wedge. Use a label or piece of tape to secure the final fold.

WRAPPING A WEDGE OF SOFT CHEESE

The technique is a little different when wrapping a wedge of flat soft cheese, like a quarter wheel of Brie. This method allows the paper to support the soft paste that's in danger of oozing out of the cut sides while keeping the cheese neat, tidy, and protected.

Step 1: Place the wedge in the center of the paper, with the cut sides of the cheese facing the lower right corner of the paper. With your left 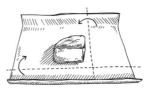 hand, fold the edge of the paper that's closest to you over the cheese, holding it snugly but gently against the cut side.

Step 2: Use your right hand to crease the fold on the right edge of this first side, then fold the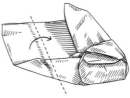

right side of the paper over the other cut side of the wedge, creating a clean angle.

Step 3: Now for the curve of the cheese: simply fold and tuck the excess paper against the curved edge from one end until you have only a pointy flap left.

Step 4: Fold the pointy flap in half to shorten it, then fold it over the small exposed portion of the wedge and secure with a label or tape.

THE FRENCH FOLD

Certain shapes and textures of cheese lend themselves better to this technique rather than the gift-wrap style above. One of the best examples is a soft delicate log of cheese such as chèvre. You can apply the French fold technique to rectangular, square, round, half-round, and pyramid-shaped cheeses, too.

With a short edge of the paper facing you, place the log of cheese in the center of the paper, parallel to the short edges. Bring the two short edges together over the cheese, taking care to line them up evenly.

Holding the two sheets together, fold them down about an inch and make a clean crease. Continue folding down toward the cheese, creasing each time. Gently press the final fold flat against the cheese so that the paper is snug, then crease each side of the folded paper down against the ends of the log.

Fold the open ends of the paper into crisp triangles, tuck them beneath the log, and tape them to the bottom of the log.

CHEESE: YOUR NEW FAVORITE NO-COOK MEAL

Cheese boards are a great way to feed a crowd, but they're not just for partying. In fact, a cheese board for one, two, or four makes a quick, easy, no-cook weeknight meal, happy hour snack, or tasty lunch. Here's some inspiration to get your creative juices flowing and your mouth watering.

CHEESE BOARD FOR ONE

Give yourself a lunch you'll spend all morning looking forward to. Pack a small hunk of your favorite hard-aged cheese and a few finger foods: apples, breakfast radishes, nuts, crackers. Well-stocked grocery stores carry single-serving packets of dry-cured sausage, olives, and pickles, which come in handy for mobile cheese-board building. Pack a decent knife to use on that tasty wedge when lunchtime rolls around.

CHEESE BOARD FOR TWO

Date night in is a great way to spend quality time with your partner while saving money—but who wants to spend hours prepping, cooking, and cleaning? Skip the stove and surprise your beloved with a couple wedges and special-occasion accompaniments, like upscale olives, prosciutto di parma, champagne jelly, juicy figs, and fresh pastries from a local bakery for dessert. Pick up your favorite wine or beer to go with everything. It takes just minutes to prepare and cleanup is a snap, so you have more time and energy for the rest of your evening.

CHEESE BOARD FOR FOUR

Good cheese isn't just for grown-ups! Take inspiration from Middle Eastern *mezze* and put out a well-balanced spread that kids can have fun with and adults will enjoy, too. Include a few cheeses, especially feta or pan-seared cubes of halloumi (see recipe on page 118); you can even serve them atop a green salad or mixed into an herbaceous tabbouleh. Drizzle a bowl of smooth, tangy *labneh* with olive oil, sea salt, and a pinch of paprika, then dip away. Assemble your cheeses, maybe some leftover roasted veggies, roasted red peppers in oil, pickled beets or onions, baby carrots, cucumber slices, juicy green grapes, hummus, and pillowy pita or flatbread. Everyone can assemble their own plate, and any leftovers will make for a super-easy snack or a quick lunch salad.

HOW TO BUILD A FESTIVE CHEESE BOARD FOR ENTERTAINING

Creating a fantastic cheese spread can be as simple as unwrapping a wedge and breaking open a crusty baguette on a picnic blanket or as involved as the colorful mandala-style cheese trays that fancy shops post on Instagram. Luckily, you don't need much besides the food to present a cheese meal beautifully. But you do need . . .

A serving surface. This can be anything from a small bamboo cutting board (ideally one with few stains or cut marks) to a massive carved slab of reclaimed wood. You could use a vintage silver tray, or a beautiful serving platter, or a big white plate—whatever you prefer. Wooden boards are best if your guests will be cutting anything on the platter. Plus, their warm rustic look goes well with cheese.

Utensils. Whatever you have in the drawer will do in a pinch, but if you plan to make cheese a regular part of your life, it's worth investing in proper utensils. They're super cute and appropriately designed and sized for the job at hand (no need to wield a chef's knife to slice a quarter-pound wedge). In general, it's good to have a spreader—a short butter knife with an extra-curved blade—plus short sharp knives or spades for cutting harder cheeses, small spoons, and long-handled forks for spearing olives, pickles, etc.

Vessels. Depending on the vibe you're going for and the scale of your spread, it might make sense to simply set out small jars of condiments. For a more polished presentation, get little ceramic or wooden pinch bowls or oversized spoons, or opt for smaller vintage jars or other repurposed food containers. The wooden or wicker serving baskets that some soft cheeses are sold in make beautiful holders for accompaniments like crackers or dried figs.

Labels. Print or hand-write labels on cardstock or craft paper, or buy dedicated cheese label holders. My favorite are simple, affordable steel pin-style sign holders that you stick directly into the cheese. Include the name of the cheese, the animal it comes from, whether it's raw or pasteurized, and the name and location of the producer.

Follow our serving instructions (see "Relax Your Cheese," page 103), taking your cheese out of the fridge to relax for at least an hour before guests arrive. You can cut harder cheese into slices, batons, or triangles for serving, but it's not necessary. If any of your accompaniments need prepping, do it when you take the cheese out of the fridge.

ASSEMBLY

- Gather your ingredients, vessels, utensils, and a clean board.

- First, put down the cheeses, leaving plenty of room between wedges. Next, add large pieces of fruit or vegetables (a cluster of grapes, a haystack of microgreens) and any vessels, like a jar of jam, a bowl of roasted mushrooms, or a deep spoon filled with honey. Arrange accompaniments near the cheese they pair with best.

- Next, carbs: long thin flatbreads, little rice crackers, slices of baguette. Add a few piles of each to different areas of the board.

- Then add cured meats: a log of dry-cured sausage, thin rounds of spicy pepperoni, or long strips of prosciutto, which should be folded in half a few times and clustered around one of your more boldly flavored cheeses. If you've got room, arrange the meat in a couple of spots on the board.

- Lastly, fill in the gaps with handfuls of small items like nuts, seeds, berries, roasted fava beans, dried or candied fruits, or dark chocolate pastilles.

Voilà! A gorgeous board fit for a feast and your Instagram feed.

RELAX YOUR CHEESE

Just as you might stop prepping and tidying to collect yourself, get dressed, and have a pre-party drink before guests arrive, cheese needs a little time to relax—to warm up, breathe a little, and feel like its best self by the time you're ready to dig in. If you serve cheese straight out of the fridge, it will have a hard waxy texture and muted flavors.

First, remove it from the package (but keep the cheese paper in case you have leftovers). Place it on a board or plate to come to room temperature, which will soften the texture and let the flavors come alive.

If you're worried about leaving cheese open to the air, you can put a clean lint-free cloth (like a flour sack towel or linen napkin) on top, invert a large bowl over it, or invest in a cheese dome (see page 126).

WHAT TO DO WITH LEFTOVER CHEESE

So you partied all night, and if you planned properly, there's nothing but a few bits of rind left over on that bountiful board because you and your guests enjoyed every bite. But maybe folks weren't as hungry as you thought, or you bought a little more than you needed.

Wrapping cheese to save for later is always an option (see page 93), but consider *fromage fort*. French for "strong cheese," *fromage fort* is a delicious way to give a grab bag of cheese scraps new life.

> TIP: Keep in mind that some cheeses will affect the character of your finished *fromage fort* more than others. If blue is in the mix, for example, consider adding only a little bit unless you want the whole thing to have a concentrated blue flavor.

Remove any inedible rinds. Toss ½ pound of cheese ends in the food processor with 1 minced clove of garlic, ground black pepper to taste, and ¼ cup of white wine (which you probably have left over from last night, too). Blend it up until the texture is spreadable.

Taste and adjust seasoning, then pop the mixture in an airtight container and refrigerate for a few hours to let the flavors meld. Store it in the fridge for up to a week; the flavors will intensify over time.

If you don't have a food processor or high-powered blender, you can grate or chop the cheeses finely. This method works best if you're only working with one or two hard cheeses and mixing them with some softer ones. Then add the other ingredients and mash with a potato masher or fork until well blended.

Bring the *fromage fort* to room temperature and serve as a dip for crackers, bread, pretzels, baby carrots, apple slices, whatever. Or spread it on baguette slices and put them under the broiler for a few minutes until the cheese is bubbly. Enjoy with a dollop of sweet-tart preserves like sour cherry jam or pepper jelly.

HOW TO PAIR CHEESE AND BEER

Beer and cheese are two serious BFFs. My theory is that this is because both are technically made from grass; the barley and other grains typically malted and fermented into beer are grasses, and of course cows transform grass into milk, which is made into cheese.

These fermented foods have existed since the earliest days of agriculture, and experimenting with pairing them is one of the best ways to level up your understanding of flavor profiles. (If you're looking for a gluten-free cheese pairing, opt for hard ciders, which are nearly as complex as wine but simpler to pair and typically easier on your budget.)

When pairing cheeses with craft beverages, choose options with complementary flavor profiles, textures, and intensities. For example, a citrusy wheat ale pairs better with a rustic goat crottin, rather than a powerful and pungent blue. If you put the ale and the blue together, the cheese would overpower the beverage. Conversely, you wouldn't want to serve a bright, lactic *fromage blanc* with a super-hoppy double IPA or intense imperial stout.

Color is an indicator, too: lighter cheeses generally

go with lighter beers, whereas long-aged toffee-hued Goudas or deep-golden blues shot through with veins play well with darker beers made with darker, more intensely flavored malts.

The general guidelines below will help you get started, but remember, a big part of the learning and fun is experimentation. Pick up a few cheeses and a mix-a-six of local craft beers and see how well they all play together. Tasting a so-so pairing will help you identify when an ideal combination locks in with your taste buds.

CLASSIC BEER AND CHEESE PAIRINGS

- **Fresh young cheeses and light bright ales:** A brew with a crisp, tangy profile will bring out the citrus notes in a chèvre or lactic bloomy made with goat's cheese. The tartness of a sour or gose will help cut through the richness of a fromage blanc or lush sheep's milk *brebis*.

- **Brie and saison:** Bubbles are a Brie's best friend. The rustic profile and fizz of a saison or farmhouse ale like *bière de garde* make them great accompaniments to bloomy rinds.

- **Aged Gouda with brown ales:** The malt-forward quality of a brown ale or Scotch ale will amp up the roasty, toasty, nutty vibes that a long-aged Dutch cheese takes on after a year or two. Imperial stouts also bring out that caramel sweetness.

- **Long-aged cheddars with fruity brews:** Got a crumbly clothbound or three-year-aged sharp? Look for an IPA with tropical tasting notes to bring out its fruitiness.

- **Blue cheese and pumpkin beer:** The rich profile of a blue cheese goes well with sweet spice-infused brews like pumpkin beers and wintry spiced ales. Chocolaty imperial stouts and full-bodied Belgian tripels play well with blue, too.

HOW TO PAIR CHEESE AND WINE

Cheese is classically served with wine, but putting together great pairings can be a little more challenging (and pricier to learn) than starting with beer or cider. When you're ready to venture into the world of cheese and wine, these guidelines will get you started.

What grows together goes together, particularly with Old World styles, which co-evolved over hundreds or thousands of years. It just makes sense to combine cheeses and wines that come from the same region: Pecorino with Chianti, Manchego with rioja or bubbly Cava.

Pair wines and cheeses of similar intensities. Serving a complex, full-bodied red with a young, subtle chèvre will overwhelm the cheese; its delicacy and citrusy notes would have been better highlighted with a glass of crisp chenin blanc.

Another approach is to contrast cheese and wine. Dry tannic wines and rich cheeses support each other because fat has the effect of mellowing the heavy tannic qualities of a wine. And salty pungent blues often play best with sweet sips—their opposite flavors play up each other's strengths.

Don't forget the role that bubbles can play in a stellar

pairing. Sparkling wines, Champagnes, and proseccos help offset the richness of a buttery, lush bloomy or a deeply flavored hard-aged cheese like Parmigiano. Pair sparkling reds like sweet, juicy Lambrusco with its regional BFF, rich, salty Parmigiano-Reggiano, or other rich cheeses.

CLASSIC CHEESE AND WINE PAIRINGS

- Young fresh cheeses like chèvre, burrata, and ricotta with crisp dry whites like sauvignon blanc, dry rosés, or unoaked reds

- Bloomy rinds with dry, sparkling white wines, unoaked chardonnays, Grüner Veltliner, chenin blanc, and young fruity reds

- Tangy, briny feta with pinot noir, pinot gris, or light-bodied Beaujolais

- Washed rinds with off-dry gewürztraminer, pinot gris, chenin blanc, pinot noir, and Beaujolais-Villages

- Hard, dense Alpine wheels with a spicy fruity rosé

- Bold long-aged cheeses like Comté or funky bloomy rinds with orange wines

- Blue cheeses with full-bodied reds or dessert wines like port

FRIENDLY FLAVORS: CHEESE AND FOOD PAIRINGS

Just like beverages, foods such as condiments, fruits, and vegetables can be combined with cheeses to create a taste greater than the sum of its parts. These are some of my favorites.

- Sharp cheddar with garlicky dill pickles
- Alpine cheese with tangy-spicy whole grain mustard
- Aged sheep's milk cheese (like Manchego) with *membrillo* (quince paste) or *goiabada* (guava paste)
- Washed-rind cheese with sour cherry preserves
- Soft, sweet blue cheese with dark chocolate
- Grassy, savory tomme with candied pineapple
- Aged Gouda with caramel
- Camembert with fresh summer berries
- Chèvre with Meyer lemon marmalade
- Feta with watermelon and mint
- Fromage blanc with juicy heirloom tomato
- Blue cheese with buckwheat honey

COOKING
WITH
CHEESE

HOW TO MAKE THE BEST GRILLED CHEESE SANDWICH

I'm not sure I've ever had a bad grilled cheese sandwich, but I've definitely had some OK ones and some that were truly transcendent. While there's not much to the recipe—heat pan, lube bread, apply cheese, flip, serve—there are a few ways to up your grilled cheese game and elevate this comforting favorite from faithful fallback to the center of a delicious meal.

THE TOOLS

The bread: I've improvised tasty grilled cheeses using hot dog buns, so just about any sliced or split bread can work in a pinch. Ideally, you have neat, even slices that are thick enough to be sturdy. Take into account how substantial your bread is—dense rye can be sliced thinner than an airy brioche loaf. Sliced bread will do just as well as a loaf you portion yourself.

The lubricant: For this purpose, traditional butter is eclipsed by an unlikely ingredient you've almost certainly got on your fridge door: mayonnaise. This is a chef hack for making perfectly browned extra-crisp grilled cheese every time. The neutral oil in the mayo provides fat, while protein from the eggs adds crispness. It also has a much higher smoke point than butter, so you run less risk of burning the bread.

The cheese: If you're using a single cheese, choose a good melter (see "Why Some Cheeses Melt Differently," page 78). Note: this is an appropriate time to bust out processed cheese, whether a block of Velveeta or plastic-wrapped singles. They're designed to melt like a dream, after all. You can also experiment with multiple cheeses—like Gruyère and a softer Alpine like Emmental, which will give you the one-two punch of flavor and texture. If possible, grate the cheese for quicker and more even melting, but thin slices also work. Aim for about two ounces of cheese per sandwich. Distribute the cheese evenly over the bottom slice of bread. (I often do this right after tossing it mayo side down into the hot pan.)

Other goodies: If you'd like, add some ingredients to mix up the flavors and textures. Many cheese board condiments and accompaniments work well in grilled cheese—think sliced pickles, olive tapenade, jams, cured meats, and thinly sliced apples or pears. As long as it'll stay within your slices of bread and won't be tough to bite through, you have a ton of flexibility. A few spoonfuls of roasted mushrooms, sautéed kale, caramelized onions, pulled pork, beef brisket slices . . . Just don't go too heavy on add-ins—you want the cheese to be able to hold everything together.

The equipment: All you need is a heavy-bottomed frying pan—ideally nonstick, but cast iron or stainless steel work well, too—plus a thin, sturdy spatula and a heat source. If you own a panini press, use it.

THE TECHNIQUE

1. Heat a pan over medium heat. Grate or slice cheese(s) and assemble condiments or add-ins. Spread a thin layer of mayonnaise on the outside of each slice of bread, from edge to edge. Spread condiments, if using, onto the non-mayo side of one or both slices of bread.

2. Put the first slice in the pan, mayo side down. Add your cheese to the bread, then layer on other ingredients as desired. Put the second slice on top, mayo side up.

3. Cook for a few minutes, lowering the heat if you notice smoke. Using your spatula, carefully lift a corner and peek at the first slice of bread. When it's golden brown, it's time to flip.

4. Carefully lift the sandwich out of the pan and flip it quickly. Cook for a few more minutes.

5. If the bottom slice of looks toasty but the cheese isn't melted, reduce the heat to low and cover the pan with a lid, which will help heat the interior of the sandwich. Cook for another couple minutes.

6. Once the outsides are toasty and the cheese is melted, it's time to plate, slice, and eat. I sprinkle a little flaky sea salt and freshly ground black pepper on top, plus a few lashings of hot sauce.

ESSENTIAL GRILLED CHEESE COMBINATIONS

- Brie + pears + arugula
- Sharp cheddar + spicy mustard
- Gruyère + whole grain mustard + cornichons
- Chèvre + pepper jelly
- Mozzarella + heirloom tomato + pesto
- Taleggio + tomato jam + crispy-fried onions

HOW TO COOK HALLOUMI

Chewy, savory halloumi is ideal for frying and grilling. Slice it into planks, batons, or cubes and sear it in some fat over high heat, and it becomes browned, caramelized, and crispy on the outside, tender yet squeaky on the inside. I like to cook it in ghee or clarified butter, which combines the high smoke point of a neutral oil with an umami-boosting butteriness. Other cheeses can be prepared this way, such as paneer and queso frito.

Use fried cheese as a sandwich filling or addition to a mezze platter, or chop up the cooled fried cheese and toss it into a salad or saucy vegetable dish. A well-seasoned cast-iron pan is ideal here.

INGREDIENTS

1–2 tablespoons olive oil, ghee,
   or clarified butter
8 ounces halloumi, cut into ½-inch-thick planks
   or 1-inch cubes
Flaky sea salt to taste

DIRECTIONS

1. Line a plate with paper towels; set aside.

2. In a heavy-bottomed pan over high heat, warm a few tablespoons of oil or ghee until it starts to shimmer.

3. Fry the cheese for one to two minutes per side, turning when you see a deep golden-brown crust form on the bottom. Remove the cheese to the paper-towel-lined plate to drain.

4. Sprinkle halloumi with a pinch of salt and dig in, or serve it with hot sauce, fruit preserves, or fresh fruit on the side.

Note: You can also cook halloumi on the grill. Just make sure you're cutting slices on the thicker side, oiling the grill well, and orienting the pieces so that they won't slip through the grate.

HOW TO MAKE THE ULTIMATE BAKED BRIE

This luxe appetizer is the way to wow everyone at your next party. Although you can wrap a long wedge of Brie in puff pastry and it'll be just as scrumptious, a complete round is the classic presentation and will bake more evenly.

Don't use the special gooey, fragrant, raw-milk wheel you smuggled back from France. Since you're heating the cheese to a high temperature, a relatively firm, everyday grocery-store Brie is best.

INGREDIENTS

1 8-ounce wheel of Brie- or Camembert-style cheese

1 package frozen puff pastry (about 14–16 ounces)

Optional: 3–4 tablespoons of add-ins, e.g., chutney, roasted mushrooms, or caramelized onions

DIRECTIONS

1. Thaw the frozen puff pastry overnight in the refrigerator or according to package instructions.

2. Preheat the oven to 400°F (204°C). Remove puff pastry from its packaging and unfold. Use a rolling pin to roll out the pastry until it's large enough to wrap around your wheel of cheese.

3. Place the cheese in the center of the pastry. Dollop add-ins, if using, on top of the cheese.

4. Fold the pastry around the cheese, starting with a corner and working clockwise, so that each fold overlaps the previous one and there are no gaps in the pastry. When you're done, lightly press the folds of pastry to seal. You shouldn't be able to see any cheese or other fillings.

5. Bake for 20 to 30 minutes, or until the pastry is golden and crisp. Cool for 10 minutes, then serve while the cheese is still warm and oozy.

LOVE FONDUE?
TRY RACLETTE

Sure, a cheese plate is a beautiful thing—but it does have a certain still-life quality. If you want to liven up cheese night, especially in colder months, raclette is the way to go.

Both a style of cheese and the method for preparing it, raclette comes from the French word *racler*, meaning "to scrape." As Alpine dairy farmers headed into the mountains each spring to graze their cattle on lush high-altitude pastures, they'd pack long-lasting foods like potatoes and brawny wheels of cheese. At dinnertime, they'd boil the potatoes, cut open a wheel of cheese, set the cut side near the fire where it would get melty and bubbly, and then scrape it over their potatoes like a ready-made sauce.

These days, there are plenty of gadgets that can melt cheese for a couple or a crowd. Here are a few standouts:

- **Barbeclette.** This affordable low-tech device is ideal for serving just a few people. Two types exist: the outdoor version, which is basically a small rectangular nonstick frying pan you put on the hot grill, and the indoor, which includes a metal box with four tea light candles underneath the heating surface.

- **Party grill.** An electric raclette grill typically has a heating element surrounded by slots for eight little nonstick paddles—one for each guest.

- **Raclette heater.** If you want to splurge on a quarter or half wheel, this electric device is the closest you can get to raclette's campfire origins. Mount your cheese in place and the movable heating element melts it for you.

Pick up some raclette-style Alpine melters and remember classic accompaniments like cornichons, whole grain mustard, pickled onions, crispy baguette, and thinly sliced dry-cured ham. Boil up some baby potatoes before your guests arrive, so everything's ready and waiting to be topped with wonderful melty cheese.

NEXT-LEVEL
CHEESE LOVER
STUFF

CHEESE EQUIPMENT AND SUPPLIES

A knife, a plate . . . you don't really need much else to enjoy cheese. But there are a few basic tools you may already have in your kitchen that can take your techniques to the next level.

KNIVES

All you really need are a couple of sharp knives, but an upgraded armory comes in handy if you plan to serve a lot of cheese.

Chef's knife. This workhorse is great for breaking down larger wedges of firm cheese and turning them into slices, planks, or triangles.

Cheese knife with holes. You'll see some cheese knives with blades that look a bit like a stained-glass window: an outline of metal pierced with small holes or open sections. These are useful for prepping and serving soft and semisoft cheeses; the cut-out areas keep the cheese from sticking to the knife. A thin-bladed offset Brie knife (see page 129) serves a similar purpose.

Thin paring knife. If you go for none of the other specialized cheese cutting tools described here, reach for a good paring knife with a long thin blade to cut soft cheeses with minimal mess.

PLASTIC BAGGIES AND PARCHMENT PAPER

You can make your own cheese paper substitute with supplies you probably already have in your kitchen. Wrap leftover cheese snugly in parchment paper (see wrapping instructions on page 93) and secure with tape. Then put it in a plastic sandwich or zip-top bag, but don't seal it—just fold it around the cheese and stash the whole thing in your cheese drawer. A small resealable plastic tub or takeout container can substitute for the bag.

CHEESE BOARDS

You can serve cheese on just about any clean surface, but it's worth getting a cute board or two—it'll make your cheese meals feel extra special. Keep an eye out at thrift stores, vintage shops, or craft fairs to find one that fits your budget. Once you get it home, follow care instructions (no dishwasher; use mild soap and treat occasionally with mineral oil) and designate it for cheese only to keep it looking lustrous.

OTHER TOOLS AND GADGETS

Once you've decided to live the cheese lifestyle, consider going beyond the basics with specialized gear for prepping, serving, and storing.

Cheese plane. This tool—a sharp cutting blade set in a wedge-shaped paddle—is made for slicing and serving thin, even slices of relatively young firm and semifirm cheeses from the top of a wedge. It's a safer substitute for a big sharp knife if you want to let your guests slice their own.

Brie knife. Cutting a lush bloomy wheel with a standard knife will leave your blade covered in stuck-on cheese and the wheel looking mangled. Instead, reach for this thin-bladed offset knife, designed to make clean, elegant cuts of soft cheese with no sticking or squishing.

Cheese paper. If you're really committed to getting the most out of every luscious artisan wedge you bring home, it's worth keeping a pack of cheese paper in your kitchen. A company called Formaticum makes a stylish high-quality type for household kitchens that comes in precut sheets and pouches, complete with professional-looking labels. For a budget-friendly substitute, look for a roll of plastic-lined freezer paper at the supermarket. It's pretty much the same thing.

Cheese dome. An elegant glass dome with a handle placed over a marble plate protects your cheese while it relaxes on your counter. You can also use it to store a firm wedge you plan to eat within a day or two, so it's always the perfect temperature for a nibble.

Serving knives. You may have seen cheese board sets that come with matching short-handled utensils: a knife with a pointy tip, a sharp-bladed spade, and maybe a little cleaver or a sharp, curved knife with two prongs on the end. These are nice to put out for your guests, but entirely optional.

Microplane. The secret to cooking and garnishing with hard cheeses like Parmigiano-Reggiano is this fine-toothed handheld grater, whose many sharp rasplike blades create lots of feather-fine shavings. Thinner shavings mean more surface area, which means more flavor when the cheese hits your tongue.

Girolle or cheese curler. Another Swiss cheese gadget for another Swiss cheese tradition (see page 122), this rotating blade on a plate is perfect for shaving thin flavorful rosettes of semifirm cheese with each turn. It's intended to be used on Tête de Moine, a Swiss cheese originally made by monks. There's a theory that the name comes from the way the device's shaving of the cheese wheel simulates the monks' signature hairstyle.

Cheese Grotto. This wooden cheese storage unit comes in several sizes to hold and age up to six pounds of cheese—no plastic or paper needed. A clay brick moistened with water helps simulate the humid conditions your cheese was aged in so that cut wedges and whole wheels always taste their best.

HOW TO HOST A CHEESE TASTING

Hosting a cheese tasting is a great way to put your newfound expertise to use and share the gospel of fantastic *fromage* with friends. Start by focusing on a single cheese at a time, using your senses to understand and describe its character. After guiding your guests through the wedges you've chosen, you and your friends can feast. Here's what you need.

Small plates and tasting spoons. If you have enough in your arsenal for each guest to have one, be green and use those. Otherwise, pick up small disposable plates (the compostable ones made from leaves are great).

Utensils. Your guests can eat firm and semifirm cheeses with their hands, or offer toothpicks. Serve soft cheeses with disposable tasting spoons, or invest in a ceramic or metal set.

Flavor wheel. This is a colorful visual representation of the range of flavors in a food. The idea is to help guests identify tasting notes from general ("vegetal") to specific ("fresh-cut hay"). You can find flavor wheel graphics and purchase large-scale prints online. Look for one that's cheese-specific.

Tasting sheets and pens. Part of the fun of a tasting is getting specific and expressive about cheese. You can offer blank sheets for guests to jot down their notes, or prep your own tasting sheet (see page 134 for a sample) for them to fill in as they go. Describing what you're tasting gets easier over time as your palate and vocabulary develop with experience.

Palate cleansers. Provide plenty of water and bland unsalted crackers or baguette slices for tasters to clear their palates between tastings.

The cheese. The most important thing! Choose four to six styles. (See page 89 for more tips on selecting cheeses to serve together.)

Here's how to proceed:

1. Make sure the cheese has had a chance to relax and come to room temperature before the tasting begins. Cut cheeses into half-ounce pieces, taking care to cut the pieces so that each includes both the interior and the rind. Soft cheeses can be dolloped onto a tasting spoon.

2. Arrange the cheeses the same way on each plate, starting with the mildest at 12 o'clock and moving clockwise, ending with the most intense cheese.

3. Before tasting, invite guests to use their senses to assess each cheese. Look at the color and texture of the paste and the appearance of the rind. Give it a gentle squeeze: Is it soft and squishy or hard and crumbly? Does it seem lush and ripe or young and firm? Smell the rind and the paste and record the aromas you detect.

4. Put the cheese in your mouth. Give it a moment to warm up on your tongue, then breathe in through your mouth and out your nose to get another whiff of those aromas. Coat your tongue as you chew so that the areas of your palate responsible for sensing different flavors can all weigh in. What's the texture like? What flavors do you notice? Does the flavor change over time?

5. Finally, swallow—and take note of any aftertaste. Compare your observations among the group, and remember to cleanse your palate before sampling the next piece.

SAMPLE TASTING SHEET

To get the most out of your tasting, use a tasting sheet to record observations and keep track of the different varieties sampled. You can write up a basic sheet, search online for a version to print and hand out to guests, or use this as a guide.

Cheese name: _____

Milk type: _____

Raw or pasteurized: _____

Producer: _____

Location: _____

Style: _____

Appearance: _____

Taste (circle all that apply):
salty, sweet, sour, bitter, umami

Texture (circle all that apply): firm, crumbly, creamy, grainy, smooth, sticky, dry, dense, chewy

Intensity: 1 2 3 4 5 6 7 8 9 10

Flavors (circle all that apply):

Animal	Lactic	Vegetal	Roasted	Fruity	Spicy
beef broth	yogurt	grass	malt	citrus	vanilla
barnyard	butter	onion	coffee	floral	pepper
leather	sweet	hay	fresh bread	honey	nutmeg
wool	caramel	mushroom	toasted nuts	pineapple	
		soil	chocolate		
		mineral			

Notes: _____

_____

_____

_____

_____

_____

_____

_____

_____

HOW TO MAKE CHEESE AT HOME

Making cheese in your own kitchen is a hands-on way to bring to life many of the concepts we've covered in this book. A simple way to get started is to make homestyle paneer—with just three ingredients.

INGREDIENTS

1 gallon whole milk (avoid ultra-high-temperature pasteurized, which won't coagulate)

½ cup white vinegar, plus more if needed

1 teaspoon salt, divided

EQUIPMENT

2-gallon heavy-bottomed nonreactive pot (see Note)

Strainer

Large heatproof bowl

Cheesecloth or butter muslin

Slotted spoon

2 medium plates

32-ounce can of tomatoes

Optional: instant-read thermometer or milk thermometer

Note: High-acid foods prepared in aluminum, copper, and cast iron can pick up off-flavors. Use nonreactive cookware made from stainless steel, glass, ceramic, or enamel-coated metal instead.

DIRECTIONS

1. Pour the milk into the pot and place it over medium-high heat. Heat milk to a bare simmer, around 200°F (93°C), stirring occasionally to make sure the bottom doesn't burn. Use a thermometer, or watch for steam rising from the pot and fine bubbles forming on the surface.

2. Remove pot from the heat and stir in the vinegar. You should see curds start to form quickly after the acid is added.

3. Cover and let sit for 10 minutes. Look inside; you should see white chunky curds and yellow whey. If mixture is still white and milky, stir in another tablespoon of acid and let sit a little longer.

4. Set the strainer over the heatproof bowl and line it with cheesecloth or butter muslin.

5. Scoop the curds from the pot into the cloth-lined strainer. Once all the curds are in the strainer, gather the edges of the cloth and give the curds a squeeze (carefully, as they may be hot) to remove more whey.

6. Stir ½ tablespoon of salt into the curds and give them a taste, adding more salt as needed.

7. Twist the edges of the cloth together to make a tight bundle. Put the bundle on one plate, then invert the second plate over the bundle. Put the can of tomatoes on top to weigh it down.

8. Let the cheese drain at room temperature for at least 15 minutes to 1 hour, periodically draining excess whey from the bottom plate.

9. You can use the paneer immediately. Add it to a classic dish such as *saag paneer*, or slice it and fry it in oil or ghee.

Refrigerate cheese in an airtight container or plastic wrap for up to two days.

ESSENTIAL CHEESE TRAVEL

Cheese tourism can take you to exotic locales across the globe or to producers just a short drive from home. I make a point to try some local cheese—or the nearest thing—in every new state and country I travel to.

FARM VISITS

Seeing where a local cheesemaker produces cheeses (and maybe raises animals) is one of the easiest ways to go beyond the cheese counter in your caseophile quest. You can ask the farmer at the market stand about visits, check a farm's website or social media, or call to see if they have regular open hours or visiting days. Even just shopping at an on-farm retail stand where you can see the animals frolicking, relaxing, or chewing their cud in the field can be a special experience—giving you the rare chance to truly see where your food comes from and deepening your connection with the people, animals, and land that feed you.

CHEESE TRAILS

Cheese-producing regions like Vermont, Pennsylvania, California, and the Finger Lakes in New York all promote travel routes on or off the beaten path that will take you directly to creameries, dairies, and sometimes even landmark-status cheese shops. Look one up on your next road trip, hit a few stops, and feast on regional cheese at your destination (or when you get home).

CHEESE JOURNEYS

Sure, you could spend a lot of time researching an itinerary for a *fromage*-focused trip to one of the world's top cheese regions . . . or you could let the experts at Cheese Journeys do it for you. Anna Juhl and her crew—including writer and blogger Madame Fromage and cheese painter Mike Geno—will take you on a carefully curated itinerary to dairy destinations like Somerset, England (the birthplace of cheddar), northern Italy, or the French and Swiss Alps. They even offer shorter jaunts to domestic dairy strongholds like upstate New York and Vermont.

CHEESE FESTIVALS

Cheese festivals are great places to meet makers face-to-face and taste their products, stock up on everything from cheeses to cheese-inspired art, taste beverages for pairings, and attend demonstrations, workshops, and lessons. Think of them like a big, exciting farmers market, except the vast majority of the vendors are selling cheese.

STATE CHEESE FESTIVALS

Vermont Cheesemakers Festival: If any state knows cheese, it's Vermont. Eat your weight in cheese, taste some local beer and cider, and then relax on the grassy shores of Lake Champlain.

Oregon Cheese Festival: The iconic Rogue Creamery hosts this annual festival in southwestern Oregon, with a Friday night cheesemaker dinner followed by two days of sampling from wide-ranging exhibitors.

California Artisan Cheese Festival: This three-day festival in the heart of California's wine country includes farm and creamery tours with some of the nation's top cheesemakers, educational seminars, pairings, and chef demos.

CHEESEMONGER INVITATIONAL, BROOKLYN, CHICAGO, AND SAN FRANCISCO

This epic, twice-annual celebration of the skill, knowledge, and dedication driving the nation's best cheesemongers is like your favorite TV cooking competition show if it were live, on steroids, and all about cheese.

AMERICAN CHEESE SOCIETY CONFERENCE

The American Cheese Society's annual conference and competition culminates in the Festival of Cheese—where thousands of pounds of hundreds of varieties left over from judging are displayed for all, including the public, to taste.

CHEESE, BRA, ITALY

Every other September, the town of Bra in northwest Italy is taken over by Cheese, a massive, *formaggio*-focused free event put on by the organization Slow Food. It's sort of like a world's fair for all things cheese and dairy, with tastings, educational events, demonstrations, and screenings around a different dairy-centric theme.

FURTHER READING

Cheese Primer
by Steven Jenkins

Cheese: A Connoisseur's Guide to the World's Best
by Max McCalman and David Gibbons

*Mastering Cheese: Lessons for Connoisseurship
from a Maître Fromager*
by Max McCalman and David Gibbons

*Kitchen Creamery: Making Yogurt, Butter, and
Cheese at Home*
by Louella Hill

*The Art of Natural Cheesemaking: Using Traditional,
Non-Industrial Methods and Raw Ingredients to
Make the World's Best Cheeses*
by David Asher

*Reinventing the Wheel: Milk, Microbes, and the Fight
for Real Cheese*
by Bronwen Percival and Francis Percival

Butter: A Rich History
by Elaine Khosrova

Milk! A 10,000-Year Food Fracas
by Mark Kurlansky